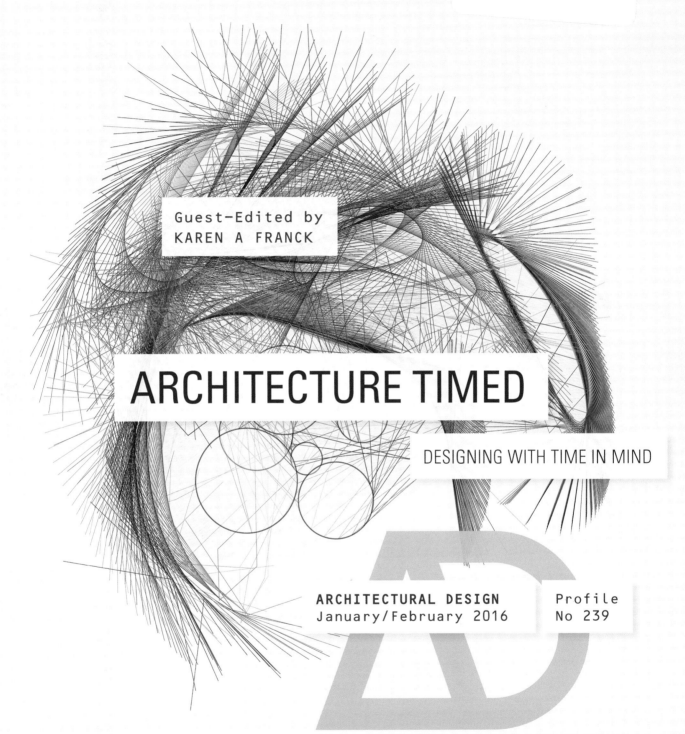

Guest-Edited by
KAREN A FRANCK

ARCHITECTURE TIMED

DESIGNING WITH TIME IN MIND

ARCHITECTURAL DESIGN
January/February 2016

Profile
No 239

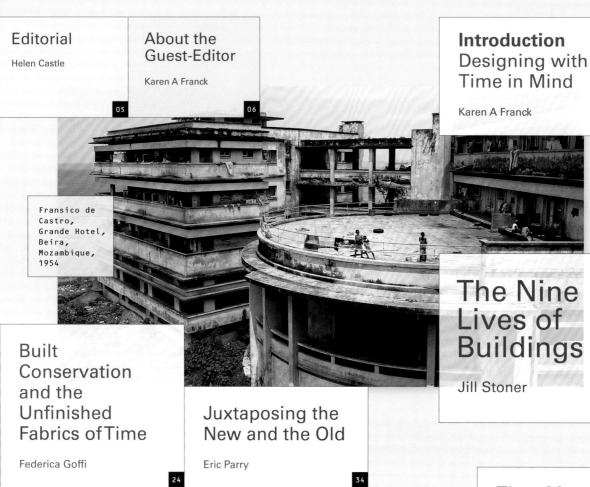

Fransico de Castro, Grande Hotel, Beira, Mozambique, 1954

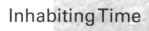

Sawai Jai Singh, Samrat Yantra Equatorial Sundial, Delhi, 1724

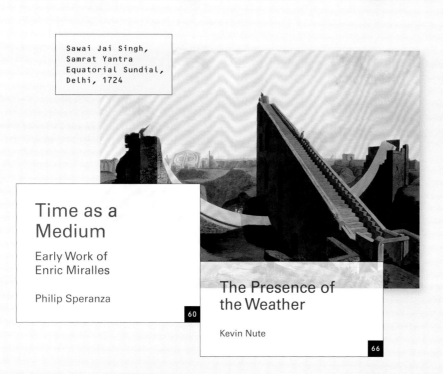

ISSN 0003-8504
ISBN 978-1118-910641

BanG studio, Variations drawings, 2012–13

GLUCK+, House in the Mountains, Colorado Rockies, 2012

Lawrence Halprin, Auditorium forecourt plaza, Ira Keller Foundation, Portland, Oregon, 1961

Editorial Offices
John Wiley & Sons
25 John Street
London WC1N 2BS
UK

T +44 (0)20 8326 3800

Editor
Helen Castle

Managing Editor (Freelance)
Caroline Ellerby

Production Editor
Elizabeth Gongde

Prepress
Artmedia, London

Art Direction + Design
CHK Design:
Christian Küsters
Christos Kontogeorgos

Printed in Italy by Printer
Trento Srl

Front and back covers:
BanG studio, Sprouts,
New York City, 2014. ©
BanG studio

Inside front cover: Brian
McGrath, Drawing
mapping a short scene
from Jean-Luc Godard's
1963 film *Contempt*, 2007.
© Brian McGrath

Erratum
In the May/June 2015
issue, the cover image of
the New Orquideorama
for the Botanical Garden,
Medellín was credited
to Plan B Arquitectos. In
fact the Orquideorama
is a competition-winning
design by the team of
J Paul Restrepo, Plan B
Arquitectos and Agenda
Camilo Restrepo.

01/2016

ᴁ ARCHITECTURAL DESIGN

January/February
2016

Profile No.
239

Journal Customer Services
For ordering information,
claims and any enquiry
concerning your journal
subscription please go to
www.wileycustomerhelp
.com/ask or contact your
nearest office.

Americas
E: cs-journals@wiley.com
T: +1 781 388 8598 or
+1 800 835 6770 (toll free
in the USA & Canada)

**Europe, Middle East
and Africa**
E: cs-journals@wiley.com
T: +44 (0) 1865 778315

Asia Pacific
E: cs-journals@wiley.com
T: +65 6511 8000

Japan (for Japanese-
speaking support)
E: cs-japan@wiley.com
T: +65 6511 8010 or 005 316
50 480 (toll-free)

Visit our Online Customer
Help available in 7 languages
at www.wileycustomerhelp
.com/ask

Print ISSN: 0003-8504
Online ISSN: 1554-2769

Prices are for six issues
and include postage and
handling charges. Individual-
rate subscriptions must be
paid by personal cheque or
credit card. Individual-rate
subscriptions may not be
resold or used as library
copies.

All prices are subject to
change without notice.

Identification Statement
Periodicals Postage paid
at Rahway, NJ 07065.
Air freight and mailing in
the USA by Mercury Media
Processing, 1850 Elizabeth
Avenue, Suite C, Rahway,
NJ 07065, USA.

USA Postmaster
Please send address changes
to *Architectural Design*, c/o
Mercury Media Processing,
1634 E. Elizabeth Avenue,
Linden, NJ 07036, USA.

Subscribe to ᴁ
ᴁ is published bimonthly
and is available to purchase
on both a subscription basis
and as individual volumes
at the following prices.

Prices
Individual copies:
£24.99 / US$39.95
Individual issues on
ᴁ App for iPad:
£9.99 / US$13.99
Mailing fees for print
may apply

Annual Subscription Rates
Student: £75 / US$117
print only
Personal: £120 / US$189
print and iPad access
Institutional: £212 / US$398
print or online
Institutional: £244 / US$457
combined print and online
6-issue subscription on
ᴁ App for iPad: £44.99 /
US$64.99

EDITORIAL

HELEN CASTLE

Guest-Editor Karen A Franck has a nose for sniffing out topical subjects ahead of the pack – long before they can be regarded as in any way fashionable. Her issues of *D* on *Architecture + Food* (no 5, 2002) and *Food and the City* (no 4, 2005) anticipated the trend for everything food; the latter edition, for instance, preceding Carolyn Steel's *Hungry City: How Food Shapes Our Lives* (Vintage, 2013) by eight years.

Time may not be an entirely new subject for discussion. Admittedly for at least the last two decades, there has been a shift in the approach to architecture away from the notion of it as a timeless practice – the architectural ideal being the perfect, completed building captured at handover in all its shiny brilliance by photography entirely vacant of people. The work of Enric Miralles in the early 1990s, for instance, as described by Philip Speranza (pp 60–65), challenged existing conventions as he sought, through his buildings, to provide people with the experience of the passage of time. There has also been much recent interest in the construction of event-driven, temporary structures in architecture – with *D* dedicating its March/April issue to *Pavilions*, *Pop-Ups and Parasols* (guest-edited by Leon van Schaik and Fleur Watson).

It is the heightened sense of speed that has accompanied the recent shifts in design and construction processes, enabled by the introduction of new technologies, that makes time such a prescient theme now. In 'Drawing Time' (pp 88–97), Brian McGrath reflects upon 30 years of drawing in architecture in which media has irrevocably changed, taking in hand drawing, CAD, animation and modelling techniques. This is a situation that has only intensified with the new hegemony of building information modelling (BIM). Controversially, Henry Grosman (pp 98–107) calls into doubt the fact that modelling has the same capacity as drawing as a temporal practice to connect design and fabrication. In contrast, Jonathan Mallie (pp 114–19) embraces the new speed that has become an expectation and prerequisite from clients, positively advocating how new BIM technologies, which enable the assimilation of data on space, time and cost in the same building model, also aid a more integrated approach in which design and construction processes are able to overlap. In 'No More Stopping' (pp 120–27), Richard Garber brings attention to the dissolution of the formal breaking points that previously existed between design and construction, identifying this as an opportunity for architects to expand their role in projects beyond the end of the design phase and a building's completion.

Ultimately, speed or the sense of speed often engendered by the adoption of new technologies remains open for negotiation and interpretation. Tim Makower counters this issue on a pertinent note with 'Finding Time' (pp 136–41), reminding architects that they need to foil this perception of heightened acceleration with the age-old skills of 'thoughtful design and measured observation'. Franck concludes the main section by bringing our attention to a significant alternative route, eschewing the obvious or fashionable. In her closing interview with philosopher Karsten Harries (pp 128–35), she cites Toyo Ito as an example of an architect who engages with new technologies while also using them to seek 'a closer relationship between nature and architecture (and thereby people)' through a lightness of touch that embraces shifts in time and seasons. *D*

Rem Koolhaas/OMA

Seattle Central Library

Seattle

Washington

2004

With the client, the architects explored what a library for the 21st century might be, in the end incorporating key aspects of a traditional library such as reading rooms and accessible stacks, but with plentiful access to online sources, as in this Mixing Room. While past types are sometimes considered to be a constraint on design, they can also be a means of innovation and transformation, the past becoming a lens for viewing the present and the future.

Käthe Kollwitz

Mother with her Dead Son

Neue Wache

Berlin

1937

An enlarged copy of Kollwitz's statue is placed directly on the floor of the redesigned Neue Wache (designed by Heinrich Tessenow in 1931, and rededicated as the Central Memorial of the Federal Republic of Germany for the Victims of War and Dictatorship in 1991). This illustrates a change in the design of memorials towards more spatial and engaging ones, as described in *Memorials as Spaces of Engagement* (Routledge, 2015), which Karen Franck wrote with Quentin Stevens. Changes in the direction and quality of light from the oculus indicate the passage of time over the day and the seasons. Flowers left by visitors are temporary commemorative markings of the space.

Karen A Franck and Quentin Stevens (eds)

Loose Space: Possibility and Diversity in Public Life

Routledge

2007

The book's essays, by contributors from different countries, examine various kinds of temporary uses of urban public space as they pertain to the themes of appropriation, tension, risk and discovery. Such activities may occur just once, intermittently or on a regular schedule; in all ways enlivening public space.

LOOSE SPACE

POSSIBILITY AND DIVERSITY IN URBAN LIFE
Edited by Karen A. Franck and Quentin Stevens

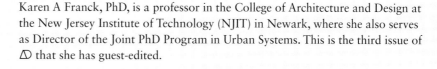

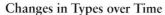

Karen A Franck, PhD, is a professor in the College of Architecture and Design at the New Jersey Institute of Technology (NJIT) in Newark, where she also serves as Director of the Joint PhD Program in Urban Systems. This is the third issue of △ that she has guest-edited.

Over the years, books on the topic of time have accumulated on Karen's shelves. These include ones that focus on the environment, like Kevin Lynch's *What Time is this Place?* (1972) and David Lowenthal's *The Past is a Foreign Country* (1985), as well as others that address time as a social and cultural construction, like Edward Hall's *The Dance of Life* (1984) and Eviatar Zerubavel's *Hidden Rhythms* (1985). However, it was only when Karen proposed this issue of △ that she identified time as a discrete topic of interest. She realised then that she had been drawing upon notions of time all along in pursuing her interest in types and temporary uses of public space. For many years, without being aware of it, she had been thinking and writing 'with time in mind'.

Changes in Types over Time

During Karen's earliest participation on design juries as a young design educator, she recognised the significance of building and other place types in shaping design decisions. Types became her preferred lens for studying how the design and use of buildings and public spaces change over time. Identifiable changes in type serve as an excellent means of seeing the present anew, rather than taking current iterations of a given type for granted. After adopting this perspective in *New Households, New Housing* (Van Nostrand Reinhold, 1989), co-edited with Sherry Ahrentzen, she and her co-editor Lynda Schneekloth invited others to explain their understandings of type in *Ordering Space* (Van Nostrand Reinhold, 1994).

Examining how architects consider the briefs and designs of past types in making design choices in the present became a theme in *Design through Dialogue* (John Wiley & Sons, 2010), co-authored with Teresa Howard. And scrutinising changes in the design of public memorials, from the figurative and representational types to the spatial and abstract ones, provided a framework for *Memorials as Spaces of Engagement* (Routledge, 2015), written with Quentin Stevens.

The Temporary in Public Space

When many researchers and theorists were bemoaning the increasing control and regulation of public space, Karen noticed its continuing vitality and people's creativity and determination in appropriating it for unexpected activities. What is temporary, although often occurring regularly, in urban landscapes became the topic of *Loose Space* (Routledge, 2007), co-edited with Quentin Stevens, and continues to be an interest of Karen's and was a motive for commissioning essays about temporary architecture for this issue of △.

Time as Experienced

The importance of considering embodied, sensual experiences of architecture was a prime motivation for writing, with Bianca Lepori, *Architecture from the Inside Out* (John Wiley & Sons, 2007) and became a prominent theme in that book. While materiality receives attention in the work, neither the ageing of materials nor other experiences of time and its passing are sufficiently addressed. Looking back, this seems surprising since *In Praise of Shadows* by Junichiro Tanazaki (Leete's Island Books, 1977; first published in 1933) was another one of Karen's favoured books about time. Fortunately, a chance to consider time as experienced arrived with the opportunity to invite contributions to this issue of △. The time was right. △

Nancy Wolf

Prisoner to a Grid

1973

opposite: These Victorian houses would not be praised for being 'timeless' either with respect to beauty or durability. But the grid that encloses them graphically captures the desire in architecture to anchor a building to a single moment in time, to prevent it from ever changing either by intention or through use or ageing – indeed to imprison it.

…no physical structure can ever be everlasting or immune to the passage of time.

INTRODUCTION

KAREN A FRANCK

Designing with Time in Mind

Calling a work of architecture 'timeless' is, traditionally, a form of high praise, but what does the compliment mean? Certainly it suggests a state of being that is independent of time. This could mean that the work does not follow the style of a particular time period, or that the physical structure is eternal, everlasting, permanent, or that it will not be affected by the passage of time. Practically speaking, all of these conditions are impossible to meet: all architecture necessarily follows some kind of style, although not necessarily one associated with the present moment; and no physical structure can be either everlasting or immune to the passing of time. What the compliment seems to refer to is the appearance of these conditions: that the work looks as if it is timeless and, possibly, aspires to be and is viewed as such by society.

The illogic of the praise – that being outside of time is possible – is evident, as is the related assumption that architecture being outside of time, or appearing to be so, is preferable to being in or of time and appearing to be that. It was in the 15th century that Leon Battista Alberti introduced what became the highly influential Western idealisation of great buildings as being perfect at the moment of their original inception in the final drawings and models that depicted them and in the subsequent construction that conformed in every detail to the original design. In addition, he successfully promoted the equally influential idea that a building's perfection is intertwined with its immutability, and that any subsequent change to the original design would mar that beauty.[1] While these assumptions still hold great sway, there is growing awareness that the aspiration to design and build independently of time is problematic and that, in fact, in many different ways precisely the opposite is desirable. So, instead of thinking, designing and building either in resistance to time or ignoring it altogether, many designers are now pursuing these activities with time in mind.

Valuing Architecture's Mutability

In large part, embracing time in architecture means embracing change. That is, acknowledging that buildings are not fixed, static objects rooted to a single moment and impervious to change, but mutable subjects much affected by every day use, intentional intervention and unavoidable material decay. In this issue of $\mathcal{D}$, the privileging of stasis and permanence is not only questioned, but alternative views and practices are proposed to widen the scope of appropriate treatments of historic buildings, to value temporary architecture and to recognise material decay.

Many buildings have more than one beginning and not necessarily a single or even a definitive end. In these various ways what is static – permanent and unchanging – or assumed to be so is no longer privileged and time is not viewed as a series of single, select moments, but as a continuous and ongoing process of change. In their articles, both Jill Stoner (pp 18–23) and Federica Goffi (pp 24–33) address the possibility of multiple beginnings and no definitive end for a building. Each chooses terms that capture the idea of mutability. The 'nine lives' that Stoner identifies include what might be considered a true death (demolition). But even then the building may be rebuilt or it may live on physically in remnants or virtually in photographs and films, becoming a collective memory. One of the 14 stone eagles salvaged from the original Pennsylvania Station (1910) in New York sits on the green roof of Cooper Union's 2009 building designed by Thom Mayne. The demolition of the Pruitt-Igoe housing project in St Louis, Missouri between 1972 and 1975 is forever repeated in a now iconic series of photographs. Or what was intended to be temporary and was therefore deconstructed years before (but memorialised in photographs) may be reinstalled with an expectation of permanence. One example is Mies van der Rohe's German Pavilion in Barcelona, which was installed at the city's International Exposition for less than a year (1929–1930) and then re-created in 1986.

For Goffi, the key term is not lives, but 'fabric'. She documents the multiple interventions in the fabric of St Peter's Basilica in the Vatican, using them to propose an alternative to the dominant approach to historic preservation as the return to and restoration of a single selected moment in a building's past. Her alternative is more interventionist, more imaginative and can extend into the future as well as the past. Time is not stopped. Nor is the building treated as a precious, inviolable object or the work of a single author but rather as a work that, at any given time, is 'complete' but not necessarily 'finished'.

Fortuitously, the two architectural projects that Eric Parry presents (see pp 34–41) are additional examples of such an approach: while key aspects of highly revered, historic buildings are restored, thoughtful interventions change them to support contemporary uses. The new is, indeed, paired with the old and the building is allowed to evolve with the changing needs and sensibilities of society. The projects are, indeed, both ancient and iconic. Thoughtful interventions are also made in more recently completed buildings where the existing structure is, again, not treated as a perfect and inviolable object, nor as the object of complete demolition, but as a platform, possibly even an inspiration, for change, as in Diller, Scofidio + Renfro's renovation and expansion of Alice Tully Hall and the Julliard School in New York (2009).

McKim, Mead & White

Pennsylvania Station

New York

1910

The main waiting room, at the time the largest interior space in the city (shown here in 1955), was modelled on the 3rd-century Baths of Caracalla in Rome. The building's demolition in 1963, intensely and widely contested, inspired the establishment of New York City's Landmarks Preservation Commission, which was able to preserve Grand Central Terminal, but only after a decision by the US Supreme Court. Today, if one looks carefully, one can see historical photographs of the former, glorious station in the far more pedestrian one that replaced it.

Diller, Scofidio + Renfro

Renovation and expansion of Alice
Tully Hall and the Julliard School

New York

2009

below right: Pietro Belluschi's original rectangular
building (1969), of concrete with travertine veneer,
was aligned with the Lincoln Center campus across
65th Street, rejecting the diagonal orientation of
Broadway. The concert hall, adjacent to Broadway,
lacked a visible entrance or an inviting outdoor
space. In the expansion, the architects extended the
original building, its materials and the pattern of its
fenestration (on the left), and then cantilevered it
over a sunken plaza with bleacher-style seating.

below left: The glass box, housing a dance studio,
extends out over the plaza, above a 12-metre (38-
foot) high glazed lobby and cafe. This extension of
the original building is oriented towards Broadway,
giving Alice Tully Hall a public presence. The building
surfaces facing Broadway are all glazed, making the
interior (and the dancers in the studio) visible from
the street and the plaza.

Arata Isozaki and Anish Kapoor

Ark Nova inflatable
mobile concert hall

2013

opposite: This inflatable, mobile structure holds
500 people for orchestra, chamber music and jazz
concerts, as well as performing arts events and
exhibitions. It has toured areas of Japan devastated
by the 2011 earthquake and tsunami. The elastic
membrane that encloses the space can be quickly
erected and deflated, and transported by truck along
with benches, stage and equipment.

Central to the idea of timeless architecture is the actual, or perceived, condition of
permanence fulfilled both by the extended duration of an apparently unchanging
building and by its appearance of solidity and weightiness.[2] In contrast are those
works whose intended lifespan is limited to just a few months or less, and whose
appearance is one of lightness and mobility. Over the past 20 or so years, the number
of such projects, often highly esteemed commissions won by architects through
competitions, has increased. The Serpentine Pavilion competition in London is in
its fifteenth year, and the MoMA PS1 competition in New York in its sixteenth, and
they have inspired a similar programme in Melbourne: the MPavilion. The online
magazine *Dezeen* displays 24 pages of pavilions built in different countries between
2007 and 2015.[3]

The open-ended briefs for these and other temporary projects, and the absence of
the many requirements that more long-lasting buildings must meet, offer invaluable
opportunities for invention and innovation. The articles in this issue by Mark
Taylor (pp 42–9), Babak Bryan and Henry Grosman of BanG studio (pp 98–107)
and Tobias Armborst, Daniel D'Oca and Georgeen Theodore of Interboro Partners
(pp 108–13) present a rich array of possibilities that impermanent installations
offer. Sometimes the brief is well defined, as for mini-libraries in New York City or
a mobile concert hall, but the installation is still either of short duration or mobile,
or both. The proliferation of short-term works of architecture as well as the more
widespread popularity of all kinds of temporary installations in urban public spaces
suggest a new valuing of the impermanent and ephemeral,[4] which at least in the
West has traditionally been of lesser value than the permanent, as Mark Taylor
points out in his essay.

What is built and revered for being long lasting, if not everlasting, nonetheless
requires maintenance, repair and often restoration in order to continue to remain
the 'same'. Indeed, in the West the desire for permanence and unbroken continuity
is so strong (and blind) that the necessity for maintenance or intervention is
overlooked in order to sustain the myth of permanence. One example is viewing the
Parthenon as the 'same' building the Greeks completed more than 2,440 years ago,
despite the long ago disappearance of the many colours that once adorned it, the
countless adaptations to serve as church, mosque and warehouse and the many other
subtractions, additions and interventions.[5] More recent buildings that appear to be
the most solid and durable may require restoration not long after they are completed.
And extensive use of stone to create a truly massive structure does not ensure
longevity: the original Pennsylvania Station lived only 53 years.

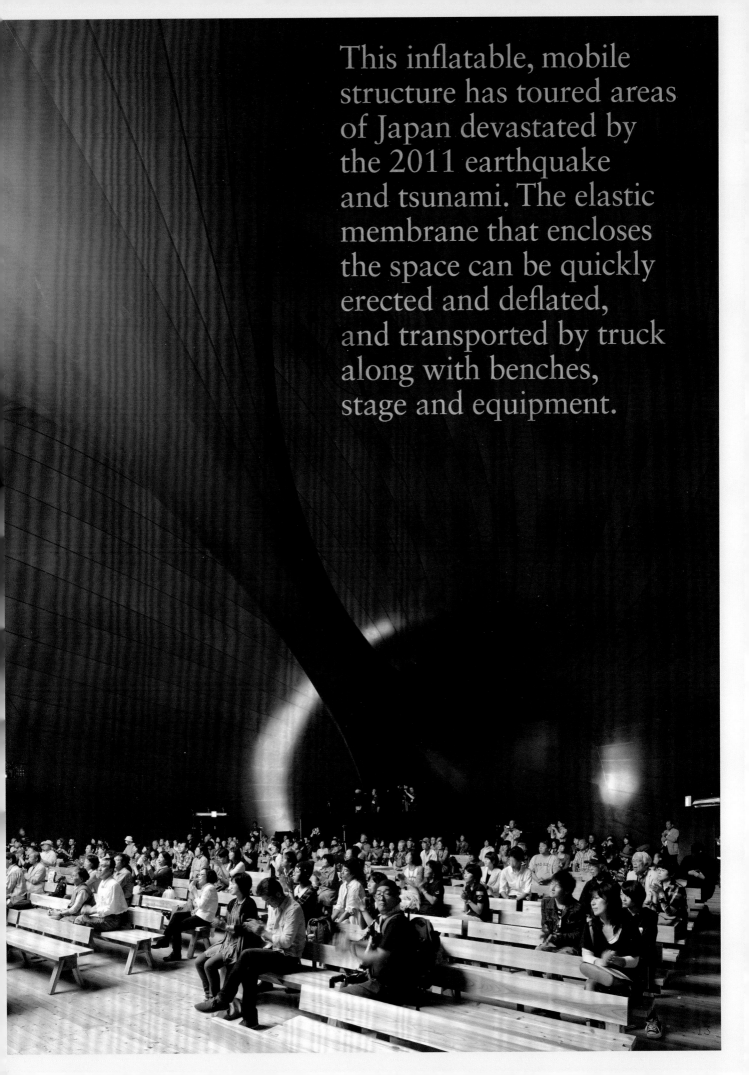

This inflatable, mobile structure has toured areas of Japan devastated by the 2011 earthquake and tsunami. The elastic membrane that encloses the space can be quickly erected and deflated, and transported by truck along with benches, stage and equipment.

Johnpaul Jones

Bainbridge Island Japanese
American Exclusion Memorial

Bainbridge Island

Washington

2011

As part of the memorial, this 'story wall' marks
the path that, in 1942, 227 men, women and
children were forced to follow to the ferry dock
in the first forced relocation of Japanese-
Americans to internment camps. The wall
displays the names and ages of Japanese-
American residents on the island at the time
and, like other recent memorials, offers visitors
opportunities to leave tributes, in this case
origami cranes.

The prized appearance of permanence, particularly as portrayed through size and the apparent durability of a building's components, belies not only possible structural weaknesses, but the inevitable decay of matter, generated by extended use, exposure to the weather, and simply the passage of time. As Philip Speranza describes in 'Time as a Medium' (pp 60–65), some architects, such as Enric Miralles, view the deterioration of matter as beneficial since it expresses the passage of time to occupants. Nonetheless, deterioration of materials can pose problems for safety. In contrast, in 'Matter Timed' (pp 82–7), Martina Decker explores possibilities for developing materials that can heal themselves, at the molecular level, from damage caused by ageing, rainwater or other environmental factors, posing an evocative alternative to the more traditional attitude that materials must resist the passage of time through fortification rather than responding with adaptation.

Revaluing Use and Experience

Recognition of the importance of time in architecture and design seems to bring with it a renewed valuing of people's use of designed spaces and, as importantly, their experience of time in those spaces. Several classic texts including Kevin Lynch's *What Time is this Place* (1972), David Lowenthal's *The Past is a Foreign Country* (1985) and Junichiro Tanasaki's *In Praise of Shadows* (1977; first published in 1933), linked human experience of time to the design of place or the choice of materials.[6] As more and more public memorials are being created to commemorate painful events in the past – another example of 'designing with time in mind' – they are also inviting visitors to make their own contributions to the site, which may well deteriorate over time.[7]

Several authors in this issue of *D* describe how the design of space and choice of materials can stimulate experiences of time. Juhani Pallasmaa (pp 50–59) suggests that, like many other aspects of today's society, contemporary buildings often give us a rushed experience of time while the greatest buildings slow time down, stimulating a sense of calm. Like Miralles, Pallasmaa recognises the value of haptic experiences of the passage of time stimulated by the decay of materials. In her article, Goffi suggests how the pairing of contemporary building details with historic ones offer people experiences of the distant past juxtaposed with the present.

Kevin Nute (pp 66–73) considers experiences of time at a different temporal scale – the diurnal cycle, the seasons and the weather – as these profoundly influence human health and wellbeing. He shows how quite simple, but nonetheless profound design choices can enhance these experiences indoors. There is no way the mutability of landscape can be avoided, but it can be exploited in ways that benefit experiences of diurnal cycles, the changing of seasons and the passing of years. SueAnn Ware (pp 74–81) demonstrates how the design of three recent landscape projects does precisely that. In experimenting with the development of new materials, Decker also considers human experience at the scale of the diurnal and the seasonal, but at a much finer physical scale – that of the molecular.

Those designers who are concerned with time also give attention to use and reuse. In renovating and redesigning historic buildings, Parry incorporates spaces for contemporary activities, such as a cafe in St Martin-in-the-Fields. Ware describes landscapes designed to be both parks and productive landscapes so that 'use' encompasses agriculture, education, recreation and simple pleasures of experiencing change over the day and the seasons. In order to meet pressing needs for shelter, services and entertainment in emergency circumstances, temporary buildings can be constructed quickly and easily, such as the projects Taylor describes. Some installations are designed not only for short-term use, but when disassembled and their components recycled, fulfil other uses, as do works by Interboro and BanG studio.

Thomas Cole

The Architect's Dream

1840

The structures that the architect in the foreground is imagining are pristine and perfect, untouched by use or time, forever empty of inhabitants. Perhaps unintentionally, Cole has portrayed the idealising of architecture as immutable, physical objects, beautiful at their moment of completion before they are ever occupied and assumed to be impervious to the effects of use or ageing.

Izaskun Chinchilla Architects

Organic Growth Pavilion

Governors Island

New York

summer 2014

Fifteen clusters of tripods, placed in wheel rims filled with wood chips, hold up bicycle wheels, and above, with the aid of steel supports, umbrellas form a brightly coloured canopy. Large rubber tyres filled with sand create a kind of patio. All materials are recycled. At the end of the summer, parts of the pavilion can be used again, either outdoors for protection against sun and rain, or indoors for chandeliers.

Treating Architecture as a Process

The paired perspectives of seeking permanence to the extent of vilifying change and idealising a project at the single, short moment of its completion make architecture an immutable object of contemplation. It is this view of architecture – a dream but nonetheless powerful in its influence – that Thomas Cole portrayed so well in his 1840 painting *The Architect's Dream*. And it is this view, of architecture as an inviolable, unused object, that haunts many renderings made before construction and many photographs taken afterwards. As Brian McGrath suggests in 'Drawing Time' (pp 88–97), such depictions of architecture during design result in places that indeed then have the qualities of the static and uninhabitable once they are built. If human use and experience, which necessarily happen over time, are excluded from architecture as anticipated, how can they ever have a place? Indeed, many of the articles in this issue address drawing directly as a significant theme, suggesting that how projects are represented before and after construction, becomes a self-fulfilling prophecy.

The dream of architecture as objects of beauty somehow magically preserved may well be related to two separations Leon Battista Alberti made so long ago. That is, the separation between building and designing, with designing to end at the completion of drawings and construction to begin only then, and between architecture and builder, with the former acting only as designer, not as builder. Notably, research shows that this separation is linked to a shift in attitude towards time: from one prevalent in medieval and Renaissance times when it was seen as a positive force, allowing – even expecting – the design of a building to be modified while it was being constructed, to one where time is a negative force to be resisted, with the sign of a great building being that it needs no change once the drawings are complete.[8]

As Jonathan Mallie describes in his essay in this issue (pp 114–19), the adoption of digital tools has profoundly altered the relationship between design and construction that Alberti preached. Not only has the sharp break between design ending and construction beginning been removed, but also architects can work closely with the fabricators, contractor and other consultants in translating the design into construction. The overlap of responsibilities and the collaboration between disciplines allows for buildings to be completed more quickly and, perhaps more importantly, also offers myriad possibilities for innovation, as Richard Garber also demonstrates in his article. In 'No More Stopping' (pp 120–27), Garber points to another significant extension of the architect's responsibilities – beyond the conclusion of construction through an extended period of occupancy to ensure that the building operates as planned, to make any adjustments necessary to enable what the building does and not only what it is.

'After' can also refer to the period that follows the dismantling of a structure. Interboro Partners and BanG studio have adopted responsibility for what will happen to the components of their temporary installations after they are disassembled, and Mallie describes the reuse of an existing grandstand in the expansion of a stadium. The development of building materials that self-destruct to become food for algae, bacteria or fungi is another kind of recycling that Decker envisions. What can happen at a future point in time, after construction or deconstruction are completed, can be explored and planned for in advance of that moment of transition. Possible future lives or other fates for a building or its parts are anticipated, and so the 'after' is attended to well 'before'. Time, as an envisioned future and a recognised past, both characterised by change, is truly embraced.

In all these ways, architecture can be recognised and valued as an evolving and uncertain process extending over time rather than as an immutable, pristine object imprisoned by a single moment. A building can be considered mutable and changing: an open and unstable system composed of flows of energy and matter;[9] a series of layers subject to change (site, structure, skin, services and space plan);[10] or a dynamic and adaptable system intended to accommodate change.[11] It has lives as well as a death – an ending that can also be designed in advance.[12] ∆

Notes
1. Marvin Trachtenberg, 'Building Outside Time in Alberti's *De re aedificatoria*', *RES: Anthropology and Aesthetics*, 48, Autumn 2005, pp 123–34.
2. Edward Ford, 'The Theory and Practice of Impermanence: The Illusion of Durability', *Harvard Design Magazine*, Autumn 1997, pp 12–18.
3. http://admin.dezeen.com/architecture/pavilions/.
4. Leon van Schaik and Fleur Watson, ∆ *Pavilions, Pop-Ups and Parasols*, May/June (no 3), 2015; Mike Lydon and Anthony Garcia, *Tactical Urbanism*, Island Press (Washington DC), 2015; Philipp Oswalt, Klaus Overmeyer and Philipp Misselwitz, *Urban Catalyst*, DOM Publishers (Berlin), 2013; Peter Bishop and Lesley Williams, *The Temporary City*, Routledge (Abingdon), 2012; Jeff Hou, *Insurgent Public Space*, Routledge (Abingdon), 2010; Karen A Franck and Quentin Stevens (eds), *Loose Space*, Routledge (New York), 2007; John Chase and Margaret Crawford (eds), *Everyday Urbanism*, Monacelli Press (New York), 1999.
5. Edward Hollis, *The Secret Lives of Buildings*, Picador (New York), 2009.
6. Kevin Lynch, *What Time is this Place*, MIT Press (Cambridge, MA), 1972; David Lowenthal, *The Past is a Foreign Country*, Cambridge University Press (Cambridge), 1985; Junichiro Tanasaki, *In Praise of Shadows*, Leete's Island Books (New York), 1977; first published in 1933.
7. Quentin Stevens and Karen A Franck, *Memorials as Spaces of Engagement: Design, Use and Meaning*, Routledge (New York), 2015.
8. Marvin Trachtenburg, *Building in Time: From Giotto to Alberti and Modern Oblivion*, Yale University Press (New Haven, CT), 2010. For a description of the influence of the 'Albertian paradigm' on architecture education and practice, see Richard Garber, *BIM Design: Realising the Potential of Building Information Modelling*, John Wiley & Sons (Chichester), 2014.
9. Steven Groak, *The Idea of Building: Thought and Action in the Design and Construction of Buildings*, E & FN Spon (London), 1992.
10. Stewart Brand, *How Buildings Learn: What Happens After They're Built*, Viking (New York), 1994.
11. Robert Schmidt III, Toru Eguchi, Simon Austin and Alistair Gibb, 'Adaptable Futures: A 21st Century Challenge' 'Changing Roles – New Roles, New Challenges' keynote paper, Noordwijk aan Zee, the Netherlands, 5–9 October 2009: http://adaptablefutures.com/wp-content/uploads/2011/11/Schmidt-et-al.-2009b.pdf.
12. Steven Cairns and Jane M Jacobs, *Buildings Must Die: A Perverse View of Architecture*, MIT Press (Cambridge, MA), 2014.

The Nine Lives of Buildings

Like cats being gifted with a new life every time they just miss their demise, buildings are constantly propelled towards change and reinvention in order to sustain their existence. Here **Jill Stoner**, Director of the Azrieli School of Architecture and Urbanism at Carleton University in Ottawa, and Professor of Architecture at the University of California, Berkeley, for 28 years, identifies and reflects upon nine possible future lives for buildings.

With supple spines and instant reflexes, our feline friends land lightly on their feet from great heights, and slip unscathed between the wheels of moving cars. These attributes figure largely in the myth of their multiple lives. But unlike cats, buildings are immobile and heavy, with rigid joints and fixed foundations. Historically, expectations were that their single lives would be long, that they would outlive their owners and carry forward a kind of cultural immortality, a virtual forever.

Yet even in centuries past, abandonment was normal, renovation common and adaptation essential. These practices were part of many a building's metabolism, but unnamed and unremarkable, and went largely unnoticed. Only when units of measure for architectural time began to shift or shorten significantly – eras became centuries, centuries became decades, and decades became years – did these common practices attract attention. Over the past half-century, time's pulse has quickened exponentially. Escalating technological innovation has produced a market economy of planned obsolescence, and globalisation has engendered rapidly destabilised or expanded systems of belief. These transformations challenge the intellectual idea of a building's singularity, its static or eternal life.

From monographs delving into the minute details of a single renovation project to technical works on strategies of demolition and treatises on the politics of historic preservation, dozens of books have been written on the practices described below. The purpose here is not to review that literature, but to outline nine possibilities for future lives for buildings, and to briefly reflect on how each one may challenge the concept of architecture as time arrested.

Consecutive waves and guises of impatience, greed, cultural sentimentality, environmental sincerity and artistic irreverence provide a catalogue and illuminate ways and means for deliberately extending buildings to a second (third, or fourth) life. The extreme conditions of passive abandonment or erasure by dynamite are the 'second lives' addressed in sections one and two. But today even the most banal buildings are more likely to dodge the wrecking ball than just a quarter of a century ago; their various alternative lives are outlined in sections three to eight. And then there is the true afterlife of a building long dead, a resurrection in whole or part, as a symbol or as a new contribution to civic life. This is the subject of section nine.

Abandonment

Abandonment is the oldest and most immediate, perhaps most natural, response when a building has outlived its intended purposes. For centuries we have simply left behind those structures that no longer seem to serve or to 'mean'. These are the majestic ruins of Greece and Rome, and more recent blighted buildings that speak for industries that are imperilled or have already failed. Sites of abandonment tend to embody the stories that rendered them obsolete, whether from failing economies, political upheavals or nuclear disasters.

The exploration of abandoned buildings and towns has become a new kind of adventure travel, often unlawful and at some risk to the explorers. Photographs of such sites have opened a new genre known as 'ruin-porn'. These buildings acquire character; they become witnesses to the slow motions of time, and prophecies of possible futures.

Demolition

Though objections to building demolition are now frequently tied to concerns about proliferating landfills and wasted resources, this is a fairly recent development. Demolition in US cities was, successively, the engine of urban renewal and slum clearance policies in the 1950s and 1960s, and hence the response to the perceived failures of those same policies. On the site of the famous Pruitt-Igoe public housing towers in St Louis, Missouri (1954), these two waves of demolition came less than two decades apart.

More recently, building demolitions have become a form of entertainment, a carnival atmosphere surrounding the event. In 1994, the implosion of the Sears Merchandise Center in Philadelphia attracted a crowd of more than 50,000 people, with bands, food and hawking of demolition memorabilia. But demolition is a bell that cannot be un-rung. It removes potential and revokes any future; a demolished building's second act as landfill offers little possibility for any life beyond its first.

Deconstruction

Deconstruction of buildings (not to be confused with the philosophical analytics set in motion by Jacques Derrida in his 1967 work *Of Grammatology*) refers literally to the selective dismantling of a building in order to keep its components 'alive' for future use. In fact, deconstruction is an ancient practice. One of the earliest recorded examples of deconstruction and material reuse is in Avebury, England. There, a linear village runs through an ancient Neolithic stone circle, which itself is substantially incomplete. The missing stones were repurposed

Andrew L Moore,
The Rouge,
2008

The rolling room at the Ford Motor Company, Dearborn, Michigan, designed by Albert Kahn in 1928. Detroit's substantially empty urban landscape embodies both the profound cultural reality of a city in crisis and an aesthetic metaphor of 'time suspended' in the emergence of a politics of crisis. Moore's haunting photograph from his book *Detroit Disassembled* (Damiani/Akron Art Museum, 2010) is a complex portrait of abandonment's paradoxical promise.

Sam Bunton & Associates,
Red Road Flats,
Glasgow,
1966

Originally intended to be a 'timed spectacle' – a global event to be televised to millions – the demolition of the Red Road Flats in 2014 was rescaled to be viewed only by a local audience. The idea of demolition-as-entertainment nevertheless emphasises our inclination to link the lives of buildings to socially complex issues. This recent erasure simply perpetuates the false promise of urban clearance as a vehicle for effective social renewal.

Charles Henry Purcell,
San Francisco-Oakland
Bay Bridge, Oakland,
California,
1937

In 1989, the Loma Prieta
earthquake damaged the bridge's
east span (on the left). In 2014 the
span was finally replaced at a cost
of approximately US$7 billion
(shown in the background here).
The original span is now being
deconstructed in the reverse order
in which it was built. Fragments
of the span, representing 'pieces
of time', may likely find second
lives in Chinese industry, private
construction and a proposed
architectural salvage enterprise
called the Bay Bridge House.

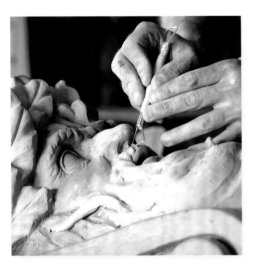

Thomas Fuller,
Chilion Jones,
Thomas Stent and
Augustus Laver,
Parliament Buildings,
Ottawa,
1859-63

The three houses of Parliament
are currently undergoing
a massive programme of
preservation and restoration
expected to last until 2030.
Stone-carvers Danny Barber
and John-Philippe Smith
are restoring the decorative
masonry by hand. Although
the project takes advantage of
contemporary technologies to
model and faithfully reproduce
original details, the masons'
sensitivity to authentic detail
is still the final and essential
contribution to this project of
'time preserved'.

*Purposeful revealing (by taking away layers
added over time) or recovery (by adding back
layers that have been taken away over time)
allow the state of a work of architecture to
remain matched to a specific time, most
often the date of the building's construction.*

for the village's houses, having offered an on-
site, ready-made supply of sandstone requiring
no quarrying or transportation.

Architectural ornament from the 19th and
early 20th centuries has been salvaged and
placed in museums; perhaps most significantly
the elements and fragments from the Chicago
Stock Exchange (1894) and other lost Louis
Sullivan buildings that are now in the collection
of the Art Institute of Chicago. In recent years,
when a building is slated for removal, it has
become increasingly common to systematically
delaminate its materials and extract the most
obviously valuable resources beforehand. As
this practice continues to flourish, it is becoming
clear that deconstruction makes economic as
well as ethical sense. Materials in older buildings
tend to be of higher quality; old-growth wood
from deconstructed buildings is stronger than
wood newly milled from younger trees. The
salvaging of building materials is now a robust
industry, and often the used components sell at
a higher price than new materials straight from
the lumber yard.

Preservation, Conservation, Restoration
To preserve and conserve suggests inherent
value and the necessity for protection from
time itself. The intention is straightforward:
to stabilise a building, to retard deterioration,
to honour both material and cultural history,
to confront time head-on and mitigate its
advance. Restoration implies that the ravages
of time have already taken a significant toll. It
requires an ambitious and painstaking process.
Whether a project attends to small components
or entire buildings, architectural restoration
places emphasis on exactitude, and on the
significance of material authenticity. Purposeful
revealing (by taking away layers added over
time) or recovery (by adding back layers that
have been taken away over time) allow the state
of a work of architecture to remain matched
to a specific time, most often the date of the
building's construction. As a strictly material art,
preservation and restoration are independent of
use.

Renovation and Rehabilitation
To 'renovate' is literally to 'make new again'.
While a building that has been preserved,
conserved or restored will likely look no different
than before (except, perhaps, cleaner), one that
has been renovated or rehabilitated will reveal
within itself at least some aspect of something
new. Renovation may or may not be applied to
culturally or architecturally significant structures.
Like demolition, it restarts the clock, but it does
so with a building that has been renewed and
allowed to remain in place.

The 'making new' will often require significant change to what is old – taking down of walls, making windows larger and staircases wider, even altering fundamental aspects of the spatial plan. It is here that competing interests emerge. A plan for renovation may bring preservationists out in force to debate issues of value, economy and authenticity.

When the issue is life safety, rehabilitation comes into play. Like the rehabilitation of the human body after trauma, prosthetic elements help to keep the original structure in place. A subset of renovation, rehabilitation is almost always additive. In active seismic zones like the west coast of California, retrofitting is a common rehabilitation strategy, introducing historically incongruent elements such as steel-frame bracing and reinforced concrete 'sister' walls into 19th-century masonry buildings, or into inadequately engineered structures from the mid-20th century. Though these elements can feel intrusive, once in place even a diagonal steel brace running across a window opening may acquire an aesthetic value of its own, elevating a banal building towards the status of 'architecture'.

Adaptive Reuse

As the name suggests, adaptive reuse is all about use. While the cultural significance of the building's original purpose may be evident in its structure, siting or ornament, very often the old site or building is redesigned to meet a purpose other than the one for which it was first intended. Perhaps the most pragmatic of a building's many possible lives, it is a strategy that can be repeated again and again to the same structure. As with renovation, preservation and restoration advocates may challenge adaptive reuse proposals. By itself, adaptive reuse is most often economically motivated, unsentimental and without nostalgia.

Some of the great adaptive reuse projects over the past 20 years are of old spaces once for industry, and infrastructure that has been reclaimed for the public realm. Two of the most spectacular are Herzog & de Meuron's Tate Modern in London (2000), where a vast turbine hall has become a gallery for temporary exhibitions, and the abandoned railway line in Manhattan that is now the High Line (by Field Operations and Diller Scofidio + Renfro, 2006–14), an immensely popular public park. Another example is OMA's adaptive reuse of the 13th-century Fondaco dei Tedeschi in Venice.

Welton Becket and Associates, University Hall, University of California, Berkeley, California, 1957

In active seismic zones, one common prosthetic solution applied to buildings with no particular historical provenance or significance is the X-braced exterior, illustrated here by architects Hansen/Murakami/Eshima's seismic retrofit of University Hall in 1991. Aggressively visible, this unapologetic aesthetic speaks eloquently to architecture's continued efforts to 'resist time'.

Once in place even a diagonal steel brace running across a window opening may acquire an aesthetic value of its own, elevating a banal building towards the status of 'architecture'.

OMA, Renovation of the Fondaco dei Tedeschi, Venice, 2015

Built in 1228, used variously as a trading post, a customs house and a post office, and rebuilt between 1505 and 1508, the adaptive reuse of this 13th–century building as a high-end department store has provoked timely debate about the future of the city itself: whether to attempt a return to a residential, productive town or to succumb to Venice's ongoing transformation into a virtual replica of itself. That is a setting in which the only images are photographs; the occupants are tourists except for a few; public life is merely performance; and the only relevance of 'time' is 'money'.

Fransico de Castro,
Grande Hotel,
Beira,
Mozambique,
1954

Designed as a luxury resort, with 120 rooms and a swimming pool, the hotel never became profitable. Following the non-violent Carnation Revolution in 1974, it has survived variously as a prison for political dissidents, a military base and, since 1991, a squatter settlement for around 2,000 people. The Grande Hotel embodies a constantly evolving pageant of 'provisional time'.

A similar unsanctioned reoccupation of the Grande Hotel in Beira, Mozambique, vacant for several decades after a short stint as a luxury hotel in the 1950s, still continues today.

Houses,
Heidelberg,
Detroit,
Michigan,
2010

In the 1980s, artist Tyree Guyton began attaching salvaged objects to abandoned houses and painting brightly coloured dots on them in this empty, nearly completely abandoned neighbourhood. This project of a single artist grew to become a non-profit organisation – the Heidelberg Project – that combines arts education, political action and individual expression. It has contributed to the neighbourhood's public presence as a canvas for 'time's surface'. But by 2016 many of the houses have been lost to arson.

Reoccupation

Like adaptive reuse, reoccupation brings new life to abandoned buildings, but without architectural plans or preservationist pretence. Unsanctioned and provisional, often socially fragile, some examples of reoccupation are especially vibrant. It is perhaps the oldest and most unsung practice in this catalogue, from the City of the Dead in Cairo to the much more recent Tower of David in Caracas, Venezuela. On the death of developer David Brillembourg, the Tower was left unfinished in 1994; in 2006 people began moving in, altering and adding to the bare 40-storey structure in rudimentary, functional and compelling ways. In 2014, the 2,500 residents were forcibly evicted, thus commencing the Tower's third life. A similar unsanctioned reoccupation of the Grande Hotel (Fransico de Castro, 1954) in Beira, Mozambique, vacant for several decades after a short stint as a luxury hotel in the 1950s, still continues today.

Architecture is most often intended to provide comfort, safety and the setting for a marketable lifestyle. Packaged and predicable, and requiring only the resources to participate, most is tepid and uninspiring, lacking the wild industriousness of the complex social system of the Tower of David, or the now lost quarter of Kowloon in Hong Kong. Even Enrico Rizzo's condemned, cold-water accommodation in John Schlesinger's 1969 film *Midnight Cowboy* offers so much more.

Pure Expresssion

Artistic expression upon and within buildings takes both two- and three-dimensional forms. These expressive interventions may be aggressively temporary or may endure for millennia. We do not know the exact history of the wall paintings at Lascaux in southwestern France, but we can assume that the caves were inhabited long before they were decorated with the shapes of animals. Unlike adaptive reuse, here there is no use at all except to call attention to a transformative moment in time.

Recent appropriation of abandoned buildings has taken many forms. In works such as *Circus* (1978) and *Conical Intersect* (1993), the American artist Gordon Matta-Clark, armed with a chainsaw, cut into abandoned warehouses and suburban homes. In *House* (1993), Rachel Whiteread filled an abandoned house with concrete; the house then disappeared, leaving its alter ego as a ghostly commentary on the decline of a London neighbourhood. In Detroit, the entire Heidelberg neighbourhood became an experimental art studio, with buildings providing much of the raw material.

With the artist as mediator, an altered building acts in dialogue with our expectations for architectural norms and conventions, as a character that serves both as critic of stodgy formulations and as a radical advocate for change. These artist's interventions are tactical and most powerful when they appear spontaneous. They remain memorable even after their time on stage has passed.

Resurrection

Every so often a building is so missed after its demolition that it is rebuilt as new. The motives for this sort of resurrection can be similar to those that inspire preservation – a desire to maintain history through the immortality of a significant building. At the site of the Arbeia Roman fort in the north of England, a gatehouse, barracks and a commanding officer's house have been reconstructed on their original foundations. The gatehouse holds many displays related to the history of the fort, and its upper levels provide an overview of the archaeological site.

Another type of resurrection, much less costly, is to build only a fragment, or simply an ephemeral inference in the outline of a building from the past, as with Venturi and Rauch's Franklin Court 'ghost house' (1976) on the site of the renowned American polymath Benjamin Franklin's former home in Philadelphia, where a simple, minimal white frame evokes the shape of the original structure. And every year in lower Manhattan, twin beams of light rise up into the night sky to commemorate the towers that fell in the terrorist attacks of 11 September 2001.

Buildings no longer physically present are also resurrected in drawings and through writing. Graphic and textual representations bring a building into dialogue with its past, and with all that building's other paper lives.

Between Chance and Intention

To some extent buildings have always had the instinct to reinvent themselves, to survive through multiple or serial lives. This is inherent to architecture. But now the questions have become more deliberative. What should be saved, what should be restored, what should be torn down and what should be rebuilt are furiously controversial issues, even emotional ones. Global frames of reference between material and meaning, between chance and intention, open opportunities for new dialogues around buildings as resources to be carefully cultivated, managed and creatively adapted to multiple future lives. ⌂

Tribute in Light,
New York,
11 September 2011

Each year on the anniversary of the 11 September 2001 attacks in New York, two beams of light rise skywards above the former location of the city's Twin Towers. Though the project is expensive and technologically complex, the result appears pure and simple – a moving resurrection that is memorable precisely because it is 'time fleeting'.

What should be saved, what should be restored, what should be torn down and what should be rebuilt are furiously controversial issues, even emotional ones.

Federica Goffi

Built Conservation and the Unfinished Fabrics of Time

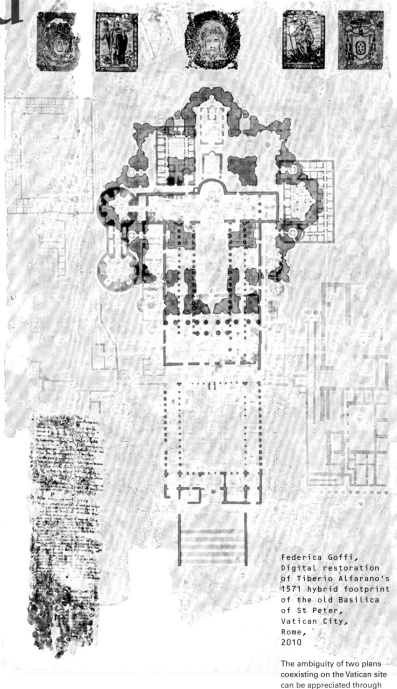

Federica Goffi,
Digital restoration
of Tiberio Alfarano's
1571 hybrid footprint
of the old Basilica
of St Peter,
Vatican City,
Rome,
2010

The ambiguity of two plans
coexisting on the Vatican site
can be appreciated through
the use of gold paint pochée
(old footprint) and an added
azure tempera pochée
(Michelangelo's central plan).

Differentiating between the static impulse to preserve and the more open-ended and imaginative process of conservation, Federica Goffi presents a building as 'a fabric that, even when complete, is unfinished and open to change'. Associate Professor and Associate Director of Graduate Programs at the Azrieli School of Architecture and Urbanism at Carleton University in Ottawa, Goffi has written widely on the topic of time, particularly taking St Peter's in the Vatican by way of example.

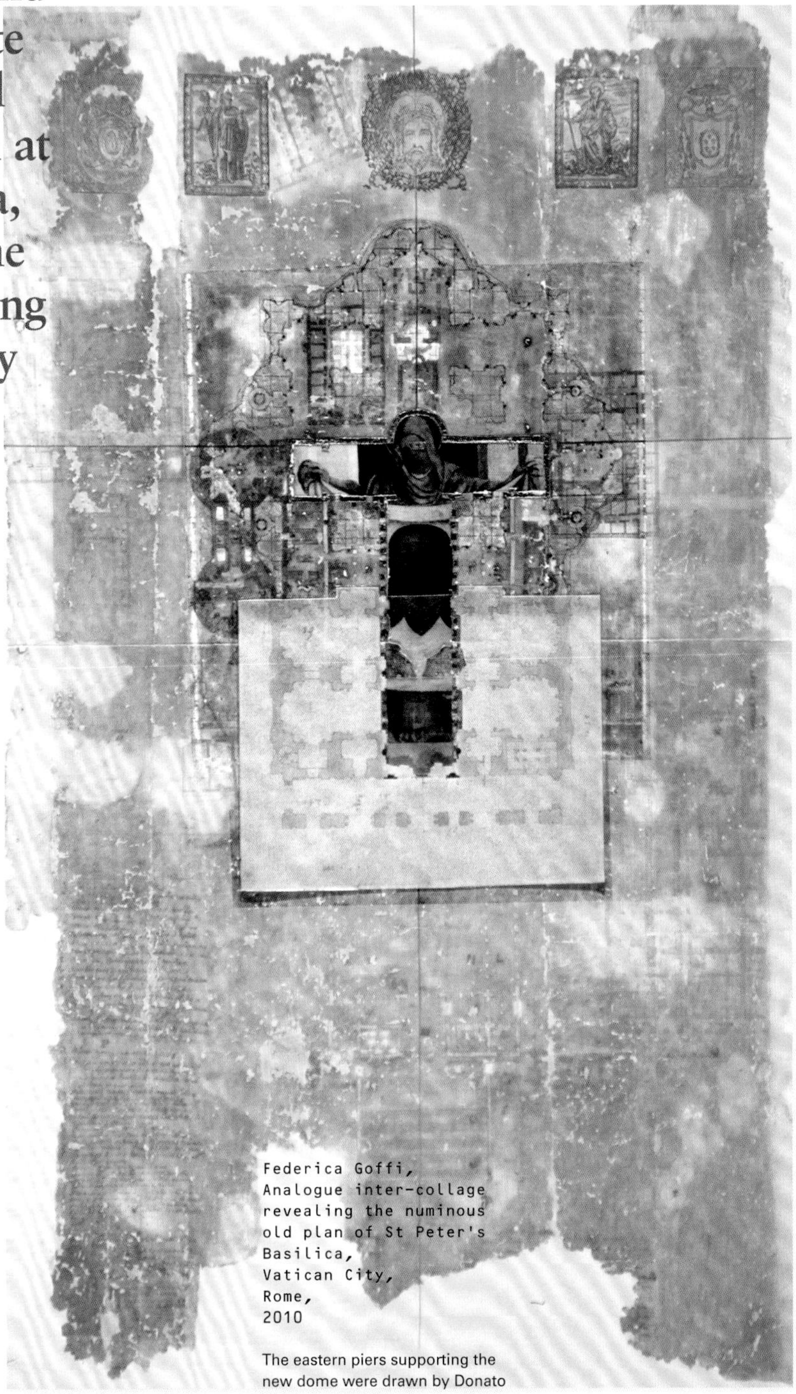

Federica Goffi,
Analogue inter-collage
revealing the numinous
old plan of St Peter's
Basilica,
Vatican City,
Rome,
2010

The eastern piers supporting the new dome were drawn by Donato Bramante (1506) to be tangential to the main nave and the transept. This sets the distance between the main piers while also setting the challenge for the vaulting of the vast expanse with a cupola.

History is an object that must be constructed, articulated, beginning with scattered traces.

These compositions neither produce nor reproduce a past or present, since at the time they came about, the facts do not yet constitute a history.

The history happens in a certain weave of traces, in a text or an account – and nowhere else.

— Sylviane Agacinsky,
Time Passing: Modernity and Nostalgia, 2003, p 52[1]

Federica Goffi,
Digital superimposition demonstrating
the Renaissance additions by multiple
authors at St Peter's Basilica,
Vatican City,
Rome,
2010

top: Carlo Maderno's eastern addition was completed in 1626. An early plan by Maderno (Florence, Uffizi 101A) is superimposed digitally onto Alfarano's 1571 drawing. The original drawings are preserved in separate archives. Maderno overlaid various designs before committing to a final one.

Federica Goffi,
Analogue inter-collage revealing
the presence of the old cemeterial
grounds at St Peter's Basilica,
Vatican City,
Rome,
2010

right: Pope Julius II prohibited construction within the old main nave and transept due to the presence of burials in this area. The cemetery portion has been cut out from Tiberio Alfarano's 1571 drawing and replaced with a depiction of the true effigy of Christ (Ugo da Carpi's Saint Veronica Altarpiece, c 1525), which was inserted to metaphorically signify the presence of the sacred burials.

Can a historically and culturally significant building be conspicuously modified and yet remain the same? This question is not a provocation, but a challenge to define a meaningful alternative to the predominant Western understanding of preservation 'as is' or restoration 'as was'. Instead, heritage conservation approached as 'built conservation' offers a means of inventing and re-imagining. Through architectural details, materials and drawings and the negotiation of cultural memories and current needs, a dialogue is created between past and present at critical points in a building's history. Instead of being viewed as a finished entity, as is common today, a building can be considered a fabric that, even when complete, is unfinished and open to change.

St Peter's Basilica

St Peter's Basilica in the Vatican is a paradigmatic example of built conservation. Far from being the result of a unified vision by a single author, since 1510 it has been known as the Fabbrica di San Pietro – a building workshop of assembly-disassembly.[2] Shifting the scale of observation from the macro-phenomena of the Renaissance transformation to the micro-phenomena of an overlooked 1571 drawing of the basilica by a beneficiary clerk named Tiberio Alfarano, it is possible to rectify certain misrepresentations of the new St Peter's as a tabula rasa construction. Alfarano was entrusted with documenting the changes taking place while the fabric was undergoing a major renewal. He wrote a manuscript to accompany a single drawing in plan: a footprint.[3] Michelangelo died in 1564; his last plan was committed to print in 1569 by Étienne Dupérac. Alfarano chose that print to be the physical support for his own drawn speculations two years later. The footprint exhibits a highly original merging of representation techniques, hybridising hand drawing with découpage and techniques of icon painting. The singularity of the drawing rests on Alfarano's ability to cross boundaries between architecture and theology.[4]

By drawing over Michelangelo's plan for the old basilica, Alfarano suggested editing his design for a central plan by elongating the foot of the cross to incorporate parts of the cemeterial grounds that would have been left outside the walls of the new basilica had the centralised plan been actualised in full. Alfarano's drawing reveals a programme of intentions that move beyond the documentation of existing conditions and serve as reminders of the essence of the old church. The actual building at that time was a hybrid formed by half of the Constantinian basilica dating back to AD 326 and half of the new temple begun by Donato Bramante in 1506, continued by Antonio da Sangallo the Younger, and later by Michelangelo. A cleaving wall oriented north–south was built between the two halves in 1538 by Da Sangallo. This wall passed through and incorporated the 11th column of the main and secondary naves of the old basilica.

Alfarano's plan, however, does not depict 'as is' conditions and is instead a 'track drawing', making the passage of time visible by bearing traces of the building's history and presence within time. Even though the eastern half of the old temple was no longer there, Alfarano depicted the original plan in its integrity. Likewise, even though only the western portion of the new plan had been built, Alfarano depicted it as whole. He thus realised in essence a double plan. Alfarano's 1571 drawing is the medium for enacting a viewpoint/counter-viewpoint dialogue embracing the continuity of everlasting time (*sempiternitas*): a quasi-eternity achieved, paradoxically enough, through anticipating the necessity of timely changes.

The duality of an old plan and a new one, drawn together through metaphoric transparency, directs the gaze in two opposite directions simultaneously, tracking layers of history above and below, before and after. The ambiguity of the two plans rejoins multiple temporal conditions and enables a dialogue between a past and a possible future, exemplifying the imaginative traction of built conservation. However, during the period of the drawing's execution, the simultaneous embrace of new and old, by overlaying the plan of the original building over Michelangelo's new plan, led to conflicting readings that still linger today: is this double plan a new design or is it evidence of the destruction of the old basilica?

It is argued here that this sophisticated hybrid drawing is neither. By drawing over Michelangelo's plan, Alfarano is suggesting that the new design for a central plan should be modified. He critiques the design, which is at a crucial turning point after the death of Michelangelo, to point out that the new plan, when and if fully executed, would have left out parts of the original consecrated ground outside the basilica, thus suggesting that changes were needed. Yet Alfarano did not offer a specific design per se; rather he created an opportunity for the contemplation of the old and new plans, drawn together to remind onlookers of a much needed design dialogue between past and future

Carlo Scarpa,
Castelvecchio Museum renovation,
Verona,
1958–75

This pen drawing on a black-and-white
photographic medium demonstrates
the physical and metaphorical overlay
of two time periods, adding thickness
to the vertical section by overlaying
a contemporary enclosure onto the
existing historic wall.

Interior view showing the
completed work based on the
hybrid drawing. The modern
enclosure is overlaid onto
the historic wall. When this
fenestration is viewed from the
courtyard, the order of the time
layers is inverted, and Scarpa's
addition is thus perceived
through the lens of the past.

Scarpa created a
micro-discontinuity,
emphasising the
separation of two
historical moments
that would otherwise
be perceived as a
seamless fabric of wall
and floor elements.

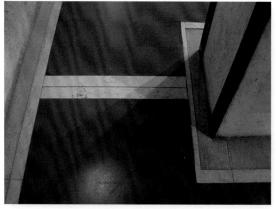

to establish new guidelines, which might inform the appropriateness of future transformations.

The hybrid drawing by Alfarano suggests multiple authorship and inspired the 1626 eastern addition by Carlo Maderno that responded to Alfarano's criticism of Michelangelo's design. Maderno circumscribed the old basilica's footprint entirely within the new. He drew the addition on a sheet of paper laid directly over Alfarano's drawing. Maderno's stratigraphic drawing made no attempt to conceal the seams between the drawings, demonstrating a sensibility in tune with Alfarano's hybrid approach and carrying on his architectural intentions.

A hermeneutic reading of Alfarano's drawing allows us to appreciate the virtues of an ambiguous representation that depicts an unfinished fabric, which is the outcome of a process of built conservation, where multiple authors enter a dialogue through a renewal process marked by multiple beginnings. The narrative of the transformations cannot be told through a single story. The plan reveals some of the contradictions and ambiguities and the plurality of voices in the story that need to be considered in order to arrive at a rich account. The kind of representation produced is very different from one that, for the sake of arriving at a conclusion, overlooks elements that might disqualify that conclusion.[5] Place is constructed over time. Temporal disjunctions between an anterior and a posterior condition can become visible through a careful articulation of seams, expressing cultural and physical articulations between building members and materials. Alfarano's drawing reveals a history that although hidden is nonetheless present. Old St Peter's exists within the new like a deep, unforgettable presence.

Modern Work
The work of a modern master of time in architecture, Carlo Scarpa (1906–1978), who took a critical position towards philological one-time restorations, exemplifies the built conservation approach. Scarpa condemned modern imitation as slavish copying with no redeeming qualities. He differentiated his mode of work at the Castelvecchio Museum (1958–75) in Verona from that of Antonio Avena who, from 1924 to 1926, in collaboration with architect Ettore Fagiuoli, completed a philological restoration of this historical building. Avena's fictitious facade reconstructions, indicative of a conjectural approach to history, create a false sense of place.[6] Recycled historical elements were reused to create a mock-up of history, creating a past that could have been, but never was. Avena's approach, fathered by Camillo Boito's theories, finds resonance in Eugène Viollet-le-Duc's concept of restoration. In 1868, Viollet-le-Duc described restoration as an entirely 'modern concept' that entails returning to one previous moment in a building's life.[7] In the process, a conjectured past is given built form.

During the Renaissance, restoration held an opposite meaning: to restore meant to give a new beginning that was to be continuous with the fabric of time. Despite contemporary revisions that favour preservation of all significant layers of history, Viollet-le-Duc's notion still holds while, conversely, the Renaissance concept of restoration (*Instauratio*) has been largely misunderstood. Continuous renewal through multiple beginnings depends upon a hermeneutical reading and a profound understanding of a building's history,[8] negotiating past and projective designs. Scarpa's interventions at Castelvecchio are closer in spirit to this approach than to his predecessor on the same site.

For the design of a fenestration system of a courtyard facade at Castelvecchio during the 1950s to 1970s renovation, new elements were sketched over the photographically captured past, revealing the permeability of time.[9] Making use of a hybrid technique of drawing on photographs, Scarpa engaged in a dialogue with the history of the building. The photographic medium represents the existing building fabric and its history. History acquires critical and material depth through a dialogue, substantiating the thickness of time materialised in the facade's layered fenestration system added onto the existing stone wall. When drawing over the photograph with a pen, Scarpa overlays his imagination on to the canvas of time. By relying on the mind's ability, through visual synecdoche, to complete the invisible gaps through our imagination, it becomes possible to perceive the old facade as a whole, even when one can only see portions of it.

Scarpa designed a building within a building, allowing the parallel and simultaneous temporalities to merge into multiple unfinished stories that are themselves contained within other stories. Scarpa's details re-inhabit a past that meets the present at junctures created by material assemblies. Carefully articulated gaps offer an opportunity for silences and pauses that allow one to move from a present into a past condition, and vice versa, through carefully sequenced

In place of a history we cannot re-enter, he laid down one we can approach through contemplation and imagination. This reflective 'tell-the-tale' detail[11] is an essential clue to Scarpa's work in historic contexts.

Carlo Scarpa, Historical *spolia* doorframe in Istrian stone, Università Iuav di Venezia (IUAV), Venice, 1984–5

Architect Sergio Los completed the construction after Scarpa's death in 1978 based on his drawings. Scarpa discovered this spoil on site and chose to reuse it in the courtyard of the school of architecture to define a resting area and a reflection pool. This detail exemplifies Scarpa's built conservation approach, which re-actualised history into the present fabric of time.

layers and voids. Scarpa's understanding of the coexistence of multi-temporalities freed him from the modern concept of historical time and its related restoration strategies.

A considerable gap exists between a practice of conservation, conceived of as an archive for posterity, and one where history is always in the making. A one-time likeness approach reduces architecture to an instant story without history. This is relevant for contemporary survey techniques, such as orthographic photography. The image in the photograph is taken as a mirror of the past expressing absolute truth-value. Contemporary electronic surveying tools provide documentation methods for the field of conservation with unprecedented accuracy, contributing to the illusion that the past can be preserved through digital replicas, avoiding the question of whether likeness is sufficient to preserve identity. This process leads to images without imagination and a past without a future.

During the renovation of the Università Iuav di Venezia (IUAV) in Venice (completed in 1984–5 by architect Sergio Los after Scarpa's death in 1978), Scarpa discovered on site a historical doorframe made of Istrian stone that he planned to reuse in the courtyard. The possibility of restoring it to its original location or use was rejected.[10] Instead, Scarpa decided to change the angle of imaginative confrontation with the artefact by converting what had been a vertical opening through which we pass to a horizontal reflecting pool. In place of a history we cannot re-enter, he laid down one we can approach through contemplation and imagination. This reflective 'tell-the-tale' detail[11] is an essential clue to Scarpa's work in historic contexts: it illustrates the concept of an equivocal space for the proliferation of simultaneous stories. Placing the actual stone doorframe within what is now a metaphorical point of entry into the project affirms the presence of the past within the here and now. The stepped concrete frames recede into the depths of the water and also time. The water's surface draws in reflection of ever-changing present moments. The reuse of this architectural spoil exemplifies the ontology of accidents informed by seemingly destructive changes that, according to contemporary French philosopher Catherine Malabou, do not detract from, but rather reveal identity over time, emphasising the consubstantiality of past and present.[12]

Scarpa's renovation projects, so illustrative of built conservation as defined here, constitute a paradigmatic anomaly in the Modern period.

His position of resistance against restoration is exemplified in the two examples cited and substantiated in his large body of work within historic fabrics.[13] Scarpa both disdained and refrained from reconstructing historical details, preferring to innovate within tradition. His approach leads to the overlay of multiple stories and authors. During the Modern period, however, the predominant focus on individual creator, rather than on multiplicity of authorship over time, has made architecture temporary, not suited to ageing well and therefore less sustainable. Buildings are often designed for short lifecycles that correspond to the predicted life spans of the various systems incorporated. Growing concerns about the survival of Modernist (instant) buildings, created in a period without history, will require appropriate answers that take into account the time philosophies that are a part of how they were originally conceived. Some of these buildings were, in fact, born finished and not just complete, and might not be suitable for changing. In addressing this task, any possibility of change as a way to achieve conservation may well be rejected, prompting instead 'as is' preservation answers, excluding any consideration of whether this is, in fact, a sustainable approach to conservation.[14]

Contemporary Work

Contemporary architect Peter Zumthor constructed the new brick walls of the Kolumba Museum in Cologne (1997–2007) on the ruins of a religious building from the Gothic period in vertical contiguity with the vestiges of a historic stone wall. But, if we were to read Zumthor's temporal cleaving of an anterior with a posterior condition in a counter-viewpoint, we would say that the old church walls, like knitwear masonry, both stitch together and support the new wall. Circular steel columns, carefully inserted into the historic piers, reach down into the foundation. New and old elements become equal and indissoluble parts of one another. By designing a porous brick wall enclosure, allowing for natural ventilation and sound transparency, Zumthor conserved an ephemeral quality of the site as an open courtyard ruin, a condition that had persisted since the bombing of the site during the Second World War.

Architectural details offer concrete representations of time. They are 'time-junctures' that manifest material and cultural negotiations between past and present, in both a literal sense, by joining old and new materials, and in an allegorical sense through the articulation of meanings. Gazing at time in a cross-sectional way, one comes to understand the cross-

Light, sound and air permeate the porous brick wall, constructing a unique atmosphere and allowing for natural ventilation to sustain the conservation of the archeological ruins in the museum.

Peter Zumthor,
Kolumba Museum,
Cologne,
1997-2007

The new brick wall structure envelopes a courtyard ruin. The original two-light and three-light pointed arch apertures have been filled with bricks to give continuity and structural support to the openings, thus realising a freeze-frame snapshot of the vertical wall ruin.

Time-juncture between the historic and new brick wall. Zumthor achieves the joining of new and old through subtle differentiation. The exposed face of the new bricks has a lower height than the old, yet it is not an exact sub-module of the dimensions of the historic bricks. New flush mortar joints seldom align with the original recessed joints. What could have become a trying attempt to achieve perfect lineups has become a playful game of misalignments.

narratives that occasionally resurface in a present condition, woven together through an open dialogue among authors separated by chronology yet united by a building's own fabric.[15] The time-lapse between additions leads to a heteroglossia rather than a unity of style. Exploring notions of hybridity and multiplicity of authorship in recent practice contributes to narrowing the gap between architecture and conservation, sustaining an alternative paradigm and moving towards defining a theory and practice of built conservation.

Today, most Western conservation strategies still assume that the best approach is to preserve a single photographic still-shot, based on the belief that by displaying photographic evidence of the past, it is possible to gain access to it. Naturalistic representation is unequivocal and presents the onlooker with a single meaning. In the examples cited, achieving ambiguity generates instead a polysemic space where new inventions may occur while fragments and spoils of the past are recollected.

Appropriate close-up readings are necessary for a case-by-case hermeneutical interpretation of the history and culture embedded in the fabrics of time, places and cultures. Looking at heritage critically requires viewing it not as a bygone past, but also as a future to be imagined and constructed. The process of hermeneutical reading is a creative one; a building's life is an endless work-in-progress. Built conservation engages current ideas of both preservation and design, blurring their disciplinary boundaries and philosophies through the construction of a viewpoint/counter-viewpoint dialogue between the aspirations of a present condition and the heritage. From this perspective, sites are considered not as mere inventories of the past, but rather as places where history is built in time.[16] Unfinished fabrics are pregnant with history and offer a substratum for future imaginings, capturing the past not as an instantaneous still-shot, but instead capturing what time offers: continuity and succession. ∞

Notes
1. Sylviane Agacinsky, *Time Passing: Modernity and Nostalgia*, Columbia University Press (New York), 2003, p 52.
2. Ennio Francia, *1506-1606: Storia della Costruzione del Nuovo San Pietro*, De Luca Editore (Rome), 1977.
3. Carlo Ginzburg, 'Microhistory: Two or Three Things That I Know about It', *Critical Inquiry*, 20 (1), 1993, pp 10–35.
4. See Michele Cerrati, *Tiberii Alpharani De Basilicae Vaticanae Antiquissima et Nova Structura (1582)*, Tipografia Poliglotta Vaticana (Vatican City), 1914, and Federica Goffi, *Time Matter(s): Invention and Re-Imagination in Built Conservation, the Unfinished Drawing and Building of St Peter's in the Vatican*, Ashgate (Surrey), 2013.
5. Bram Kempers, 'Diverging Perspectives: New Saint Peter's – Artistic Ambitions, Liturgical Requirements, Financial Limitations and Historical Interpretations', *Mededelingen van het Nederlands Instituut te Rome*, 55, 1996, pp 213–51.
6. Richard Murphy, *Carlo Scarpa and the Castelvecchio*, Butterworth (Oxford), 1990, and Francesco Dal Co and Giuseppe Mazzariol, *Carlo Scarpa: The Complete Works*, Electa (Milan), 1985.
7. Eugène Emmanuel Viollet-le-Duc, *The Foundations of Architecture: Selections From the Dictionnaire Raisonné* [1868], George Braziller (New York), 1990.
8. Arnaldo Bruschi, Christoph Luitpold Frommel, Franz Wolff Metternich and Christof Thoenes, *San Pietro che non c'è*, Electa (Milan), 1996, pp 281–303.
9. Federica Goffi, 'Carlo Scarpa and the Eternal Canvas of Silence', *ARQ*, 10 (3–4), 2006, pp 291–300.
10. Sergio Los, *Verum Ipsum Factum, Il Progetto di Carlo Scarpa per l'Ingresso dell'Istituto Universitario di Architettura di Venezia*, Culva (Venice), 1985 pp 90–91.
11. Marco Frascari, 'The Tell-the-Tale Detail', *VIA*, 7, 1984, pp 22–37.
12. Catherine Malabou, *The Ontology of the Accident: An Essay on Destructive Plasticity*, Polity (Cambridge), 2009, pp 1–6.
13. The transcriptions of Scarpa's lectures at the IUAV recently published by Franca Semi in *A Lezione con Carlo Scarpa*, Cicero (Venice), 2010, pp 56–7, bear witness to his disapproval of restoration, which should be attempted only under unique circumstances and with special care. He also pointed to the necessity not merely to respect the past, but also to be critical of it.
14. Mark Crinson, *Urban Memory: History and Amnesia in the Modern City*, Routledge (London), 2005.
15. George Kubler, *The Shape of Time: Remarks on the History of Time*, Yale University Press (New Haven, CT), 1962, pp 1–4, 28–30, 96–9.
16. David Leatherbarrow and Mohsen Mostafavi, *On Weathering: The Life of Buildings in Time*, MIT Press (Cambridge, MA), 1993.

Juxtaposing the New

The reputation of the renowned London-based architect **Eric Parry** rests on his contemporary, but highly contextual approach to the designing of buildings in historic and highly visible city-centre sites. The author of *Context: Architecture and the Genius of Place* (Wiley, 2015), Parry acknowledges here the debt that he owes to the thinking of Dalibor Vesely, while describing how it plays out in his renewal project for St Martin-in-the-Fields in London and the extension of the Holburne Museum in Bath.

Eric Parry,
'Necropolis',
St Giles,
London,
1979

Axonometric from Dalibor Vesely, *Architecture and Continuity*, 1982, p 14. 'The goal of the project was not to design a cemetery per se, but to establish a territory in the centre of the city which will be a permanent symbol of its destiny.'

Eric Parry

AND
THE OLD

To avoid the meaninglessness of
the contemporary city it is not
necessary to search for some ideal
order in the preindustrial past.
It is possible to start from the
given reality of any existing city
and to discover, in most of them,
a residuum of tradition sufficient
to support a consistent imaginative
and sometimes even radical
reinterpretation of the status quo.

— Dalibor Vesely, *Architecture and
Continuity*, Themes Series, Architectural
Association (London), 1982, p 12[1]

When Dalibor Vesely advocated the value of continuity for the contemporary city in the early 1980s at the Architectural Association (AA) School of Architecture in London, he was a brave, lone voice in the company of his avant-garde peers. Unit leaders at the time included Peter Cook, Zaha Hadid, Rem Koolhaas, Daniel Libeskind and Bernard Tschumi, who were largely focused on innovative form-finding and a clean break with tradition. The student projects in Vesely's 1982 publication *Architecture and Continuity* mainly concerned the ambitious reconfiguration of a post-industrial site adjacent to Kentish Town High Street in North London. In the intervening decades, the positions of Vesely's well-known contemporaries at the AA have been played out and developed with significant impact on the architectural and urban world today.

It was Vesely's broad understanding of the continuities of European tradition, though, that informed his instinct for continuity, and led him to propose a rich topography of urban adjacencies and spatial configuration at odds with the other prevalent formalistic tendencies. Two thematic issues that played an important part in *Architecture and Continuity* have re-emerged in two of my own projects in particular – the renovation of St Martin-in-the-Fields, London (2001–08), and the Holburne Museum in Bath, Somerset (2002–11). The first concerned the critical issue of the sacred, the second that of the pleasure garden, and both the role of poetics in the contemporary city. Here I intend to describe some of the design intent of both projects as an illustration of an approach to the reinvigoration of historic fabric through the dialogue between new and old.

Eric Parry Architects,
St Martin-in-the-Fields renewal project,
Trafalgar Square, London,
2001-8

View westwards of the completed project with the widened Church Path accommodating in the foreground the granite balustrade to the lightwell, and in the distance the glass-walled entry pavilion set between James Gibbs's Portland stone masterpiece (1726) with the addition of Shirazeh Houshiary and Pip Horney's east window (2008); and John Nash's stuccoed north range.

below top: The historical sequence of plans, redrawn in 2011. Left: Gibbs's church and crypt (completed in 1726) inserted into the dense urban fabric and burial grounds, on the site of the Tudor church once set in the 'Fields'. Centre: Nash exposed the church as a key element at the northeast corner of his public space, later called Trafalgar Square. He designed the north terrace combining a vicarage, vestry and school building, and replaced the burial grounds with brick vaults to house coffins below the school playground. Right: The reordered public realm of the renewal project with an entry pavilion and lightwell placed in the space conjured between Gibbs's and Nash's buildings.

below bottom: East–west section of the newly formed public realm below the reconfigured Church Path. From the east (left) are the Dick Sheppard Chapel, lightwell, Church Hall, exhibition space with crypt restaurant beyond, pavilion and shop.

View from the subterranean cloistered space from which the simultaneity of the whole is realised: the chapel behind the viewer; the Chinese congregation meeting hall and parish to the left (with the music recital hall beyond); the new Church Hall and the exhibition spaces ahead. Above and to the right is the window to The Connection at St Martin-in-the-Fields. Above the lightwell, the body of the church is seen from the third historical perspective.

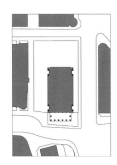
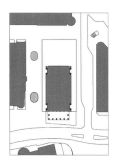

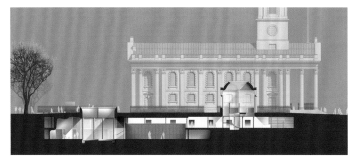

The subterranean lightwell from the crypt-level basement with the entrance to the Dick Sheppard Chapel at centre.

The Dick Sheppard Chapel. Lateral light from the lightwell is mediated by the vertical fins of the west hall. The altar is of French limestone from a quarry close to the First World War battlefront. The backdrop is a Gerhard Richter tapestry with top light from the pavement above.

St Martin-in-the-Fields

The St Martin-in-the-Fields renewal project is the most recent of the repeated insertions of the new into the old, on ground that has maintained its cultural purpose as a place of sanctuary for 1,600 years. In the 18th century James Gibbs swept away a tottering Tudor structure and replaced it with his much-copied Baroque church. In the 19th century John Nash created the urban set piece around Gibbs's church as part of his monumental London plan. But however brilliant was Nash's stage set, his burial vaults were a failure that oozed putrefaction, leading to their early closure.

The parish community is complex, and in parallel to the architectural framework of our project, radical social adjustments took place: for example, two organisations focused on the homeless were integrated as one, now named The Connection at St Martin-in-the-Fields, which has become a leading authority nationally in social reintegration. Also, while world-famous for its choir music, musicians and the Academy, there was no rehearsal space or adequate facilities even for changing. Many of the 30 services a week, in several languages, were held in highly compromised settings epitomised by the confused configuration of the east end of the church. Generally, circulation was tortured and overlapping, and with services failing and roofs leaking, the whole was, both literally and metaphorically, a sinking ship.

There is not space enough in this article to expand on the complex social and architectural history of the church and its urban setting, but in summary the three plans illustrated here show the changing condition. In the design of the new, mainly subterranean spaces that bind the 18th- and 19th-century buildings together, the spatial configuration synthesised four particular territories: horizon, light, simultaneity and material.

It was an unwritten rule of the architectural competition for the renewal project that most of the brief would have to be accommodated below ground; the adage 'three's a crowd' applied to the site of approximately 60 x 80 metres (197 x 262 feet) centred around Gibbs's masterpiece and Nash's urban setting. It was also true that to create usable space out of what the vicar, Nicholas Holtam, described as that 'designed for the dead but used by the living', all of Nash's constraining vaults would need to be swept away. The echo of precedents, never literal flicker – the interiority of the Domus Aurea, Rome; the terror of the labyrinth and Theseus's ball of string; the lower world of the Place des Martyrs, Brussels and the Nymphaeum at the Villa Giulia, Rome.

In cutting back Nash's railings along Church Path (themselves a copy of Gibbs's) to create space for a pavilion to house a stairway and lift, my initial intention was that it should be cubic, made of granite baulks laid as a grid with a lining of glass. This positive cube, sat on the sectional line of the ground, could then be balanced by its negative – set into the ground – to admit light and air and, most importantly, to create a focus 40 metres (130 feet) underground as one descends the stairway to the level of Gibbs's church crypt. A second, lower level allowed the generosity of three double-height spaces for collective use: one a church hall, one a music rehearsal space, and the third the subterranean gathering or cloister from which the simultaneity of the whole is realised.

On my first invited tour of the whole site at the time of the competition, I was reminded later by Nick Holtam, I had opined that the project was as much about the iconography of light as about spatial and material order. The most magnificent contemporary manifestation's are Shirazeh Houshiary and Pip Horne's east window (2008) and altar (2011), which have induced the contribution of other great artists such as Gerhard Richter, that syncopate the ordering by light of the sacred passage from the shadows of the west to the brilliance of the east. This journey is paralleled in the new spaces below ground from the entrance pavilion to the crypt level, where at the landing there are views across the church hall to the light of the subterranean cloister. The sectional journey culminates in the small side-lit chapel dedicated to Dick Sheppard, vicar during the years of the First World War, who established the crypt as a place of refuge for soldiers coming and going from Charing Cross station and for the homeless. The wide-ranging spatial and social uses and their proximities make this project a very pertinent example of ideas expounded by Vesely – particularly those of the typicality of situation, the simultaneity of parts and reverberance of the whole.

There is also scope for interpretation of the project materially, from stone to stucco, metal to glass and the enveloping warmth of wood. One instance illustrates a little of this line of thought. Prior to the project, Vesely had given me a copy of Roger Caillois's *The Writing of Stones*.[2] In Marguerite Yourcenar's introduction to the book she reminds us of Caillois's brilliant observation of the quality of crystal as being 'like souls casting no shadows'[3] – an idea that led me to the glass walls of the pavilion set between Nash and Gibbs.

While this radical reordering created two fine, superimposed double-height rooms – it also created two myopic urban blunders.

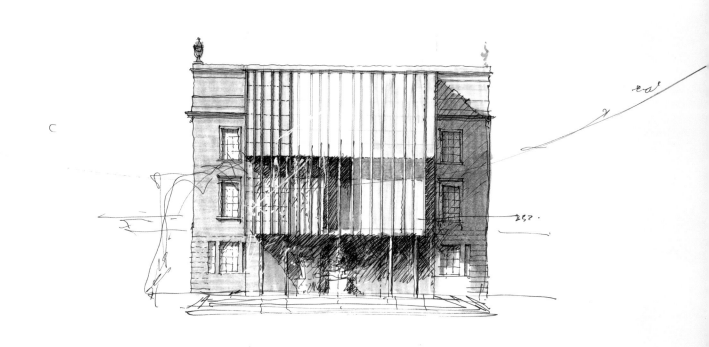

Eric Parry,
Renewal of the Holburne Museum,
Bath, first studies drawings,
2004

above and left: Elevation studies of the double-sided (city/garden) building characters. Facing the city, stone upon stone, from the lightness of the urns to the weight of the rusticated base; facing the garden, the sheer glass base rising to the weight of the blind gallery wall of the top floor.

John Nixon,
Sydney Hotel and Gardens,
Bath,
Somerset,
1801

Watercolour showing the rear of the Sydney Hotel six years after the pleasure gardens opened.

The Holburne Museum

The reordering and extension to the Holburne Museum in Bath is in several ways an interesting corollary to the renewal of the St Martin-in-the-Fields project. One concerns the sacred at the heart of its metropolitan setting, the other play in an urban garden. While both involve the ceremony of entry, one is defined by liturgy and shelter, and the other by display and spectacle; one is a sun that radiates its effect, the other a lens on a linear axis; one is about descent to a subterranean complex, the other about rising to a floating cave. Both have the commonality of wonder and conviviality and invite participation; the sites have been awoken from a somnambulant struggle with their pre-existing fabric by physical change and social reordering. Coincidentally, both were designed in parallel, chronologically, and had to deal with broad scrutiny, some severe criticism, tight fiscal constraints and determined supportive clients.

The art museum building is the kernel of a remarkable survivor, the Sydney Gardens – the only extant outline of an 18th-century pleasure garden in Britain. Its heyday preceded the arrival of the railway, both physically as Isambard Kingdom Brunel's Great Western Line literally ploughed its way through the centre of the garden in 1840, and psychologically because amusement could forever after be found further afield. The scale of the gardens, at approximately 200 metres (650 feet) wide by 360 metres (1,180 feet) in length, is similar to that of the great pleasure gardens of London, but it was conceived most inventively as a (lozenge-shaped) space bordered by terraced houses separated by a road, and bound by a ride on which one needs to imagine strutting horses and fashionable riders.

Once through the Sydney Hotel, which served as the entry, gaming rooms and, presumably, accommodations, the gardens offered an extraordinary spectacle, evocatively illustrated in John Nixon's 1801 watercolour of the site, which gives a vivid impression of them in full tilt, orchestra over the threshold, supper boxes, swings, a labyrinth, and the complex layered, ascending landscape. However, the garden-facing facade was muted and cut off from its garden life by the architectural modifications executed by the trustees of the William Holburne bequest, to house his collection and to accommodate a director and caretaker on the ground floor. While this radical reordering created two fine, superimposed double-height rooms – the upper a top-lit picture gallery, the lower a nine-windowed ballroom with magnificent views down Great Pulteney Street – it also created two myopic urban blunders. The first was the closure of the axis leading from the city centre to the gardens due to the placement of the main stairway on this axis to deflect public energy upwards into the new rooms, and the second was the building of an enclosing wall to the rear marking the new boundary between the private museum and public gardens.

My initial sketches for the architectural competition addressed the latent power of the garden context, with the new extension building hovering above the restored transparency of the garden at ground level. The central stairway was moved and reconfigured to open the axis to the garden once more and to provide a central point of invigilation. The architectural proposal in plan and section was driven both by a clear curatorial need for a new temporary exhibition space to be at the same level as the existing top-lit picture gallery on the second floor, and the economic necessity of running a small museum with limited resources. The essential core of the permanent exhibition – the Holburne collection, domestic in scale and diverse in its parts – was previously lost in the first-floor ballroom, set in formally arranged Victorian vitrines. In the new extension it was possible to compose a three-dimensionally responsive set of spaces by creating two floors within the first-floor sectional dimensions of the existing building, with axial and diagonal views to the garden, where the exhibits are not light sensitive, such as porcelain, and darker areas for miniatures and furniture. At the centre is a double-height void that is set at the lower level, very much as it would have been found in Holburne's town house in Cavendish Crescent, Bath, as known from the detailed inventory made following his death. The new top-lit temporary exhibition space is housed at second-floor level with tall blind walls.

Externally, the manifestation of the uses of the new extension created the inverse of the existing stone building, which in traditional character rises from the heavy rustication of the base to the lightness of the urns breaking the silhouette. Our brief required the largest un-punctured walls at the top and as full a transparency as possible for the garden room cafe at ground level. The preliminary elevation sketch was a response to the massing, showing the idea of a dialogue between glass and glazed faience, with a tripartite ordering to the wall: faience on the wall of the top-lit gallery; a faience wall behind an outer glass veil to the intermediate level; and an environmental glass wall behind the outer glass veil at the ground level. Set within the foliate surroundings of mature trees, the intention was to develop an ambiguity of surface reflection, multiplied at the ground and first floors by the layering created by the 800-millimetre (31½-inch) space between the double skin. The theatricality of the interspersed solid and glazed panels creates several levels of ambiguity, the first of which is the virtual levitation of the building. The structure reinforces this with the body of the building being propped at three of its corners with paired cruciform piers constructed from rolled plate sections, and held off the corners.

The second level of ambiguity is manifest in the articulation of the building. As the preliminary sketch shows, I did not want the surface to be revealed as a grid of ceramic tiles. The suppression of the vertical joint was made by a rhythm of unequal widths, and by the placing of vertical fins over the joints that would become like hanging tendrils, and the support for the veil of outer glass below. At the garden level, the external veil of glass panels, relieved of the duty of air-tightness, are separated by a 40-millimetre (approximately 1½-inch) ventilating joint.

The third level of ambiguity concerns the materiality of the whole. Through a long gestation period, many glazes were developed for the ceramic, all single-fired double layering,

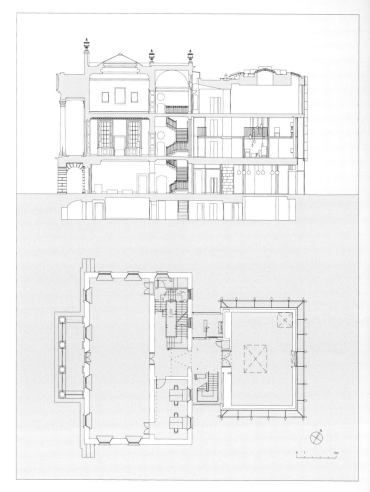

The theatricality of the interspersed solid and glazed panels creates several levels of ambiguity, the first of which is the virtual levitation of the building.

Eric Parry Architects,
Holburne Museum
extension,
Bath,
Somerset,
2011

opposite: Longitudinal section and
first-floor plan (redrawn in 2014).
Section from city (left) to garden
(right), with the existing building
and relocated stairway city-facing,
and the new extension to the
garden replicating the original
Janus-headed condition – the
gravity of the one and levity of the
other.

above: The foliate garden setting
kinetic in the reflective materials of
the new facade.

Notes
1. Dalibor Vesely, *Architecture and Continuity*, Themes
Series, Architectural Association (London), 1982, p 12.
2. Roger Caillois, *The Writing of Stones*, University
Press of Virginia (Charlottesville, VI), 1985.
3. Marguerite Yourcenar, 'Introduction', in *ibid*, p xix.

beginning with a deep olive-green layer of manganese
and a stippled titanium oxide white overlayer. The material
combination of formed ceramic with a dapple high glaze on
rounded surfaces, the multiple reflection of glass on ceramic
and glass on glass, coupled with the animation caused by
the wind in the trees and the pulse of light and shadow,
render the whole as responsive and mysterious as intended,
particularly at dusk, like an image I held in my mind from my
first visit to the Holburne of René Magritte's 'The Empire of
Lights' series of oil paintings (1953–4), in anticipation of the
dormant beauty of the gardens to be rekindled.

Both the St Martin-in-the-Fields and Holburne Museum
projects benefited from substantial grant aid that in turn
required strict predictive assessments of their social and
financial viability. From these we are now able to reflect
accurately on the results, which have in both cases been
phenomenal in terms of use, cultural remit and now
future potential, all unthinkable before the architectural
interventions and additions. Vesely's vision of an 'imaginative
and sometimes even radical reinterpretation of the status
quo' has been played out through projects as diverse as
Herzog & de Meuron's Tate Modern in London (2000) and
David Chipperfield's Neues Museum in Berlin (2009) , but
where he was particularly ahead of his time was in his
thinking about the dialogue between the part and the whole,
a reverberation with the city at its core. ᗺ

Time
Matters

Kengo Kuma & Associates,
T-Room,
21st Century Museum of Contemporary Art,
Kanazawa,
Ishikawa Prefecture,
Japan,
2005

The entrance opening expands and contracts in periodic
cycles inviting the visitor to judge how and when they enter
the space in order to receive their respective cup of tea.

Mark Taylor

Transition and
Transformation
in Architecture

Though the contemporary world in the West has only just started to value architecture that is temporary and highly flexible rather than permanent and timeless, the East has a long building tradition respecting the transitory and ephemeral. **Mark Taylor**, Professor of Architecture at the University of Newcastle, Australia, looks at ways in which recent architecture in China, Japan and New Zealand has been embracing the limits and passing of time.

The architecture traditions of the West have generally evolved around load-bearing monumentality where apparent permanence, without modification, has long been prized. Within this tradition the idea of 'timeless' is frequently used as a term of high praise. One could say that much of the historical tradition of Western architecture is formed through principles of Newtonian mechanics and Euclidian geometry, in which temporal relations and the continuum of numbers are unified. In this paradigm, time becomes subordinate to space and spatial models.

Other traditions such as those in the East, which evolved primarily through frame structures, regard the ephemeral and the changeable with similar respect, and are recognised as important aspects of architecture. In this historical tradition, localised climate conditions affect seemingly impermanent building materials, such as perishable organic plant materials, that are both readily accessible and require regular maintenance or replacement. Such differences between East and West were observed by the 19th-century traveller Edward Morse, who noted that in Japanese houses there were no 'permanently enclosed rooms [and] the whole side of a house may be flung open to sunlight and air'.[1] The shock of this dissimilarity, suggests Morse, is that 'an Englishman … recognizes little merit in the frail and perishable nature of these structures', and fails to see architecture from their cultural standpoint. Moreover, while replacing fragile building materials might be necessary for continued weather protection, in some instances the reconstruction of architecture is a deliberate cultural act. One noteworthy example of this rebuilding practice is the Ise Shrine in Mie Prefecture, Japan, which is re-created on a 20-year cycle, and suggests the evolution of a 'different philosophical understanding of historical value that does not primarily interface with material and form, but rather with time and place'.[2]

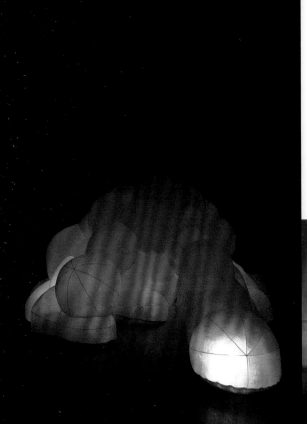

Kengo Kuma & Associates, T-Room, 21st Century Museum of Contemporary Art, Kanazawa, Ishikawa Prefecture, Japan, 2005

left: The tearoom is made from a translucent membrane structure filled with air that moves by inflating and deflating the air pressure.

right: Visitors locate themselves inside the expanding and contracting tearoom through tactile interaction, which suggests a more intimate relationship between architecture, people and sociability.

The Passing of Time

The ability to see architecture from different perspectives or as an object affected by a range of external parameters that includes time, seasonal change, daily activities and so on, indicates that a house/object might be a transformative entity. That is, objects may, as Bernard Cache observes, no longer be defined as fixed entities, but exist in a state of constant transformation.[3] He argues that 'form' is not the result of formal eccentricity, but rather the product of more pliant, fluid, complex and heterogeneous means of practice. This change in Western thought enables shared concepts to adjust such that 'time' is now inherently bound to design, in the manner that an entity establishes dynamic associations with its environment as well as within itself. That is, it opens space for the transitory and transformative to resist traditional paradigms and ideologies, something that architect and theorist Vittorio Gregotti also foreshadowed. He observed how the West has engaged transformative tensions expressed through new objects that 'move and divide rather than interpret',[4] suggesting that they are active rather than passive entities.

One recent project in the East that engages this debate is the T-Room designed by Japanese architect Kengo Kuma for the 'Alternative Paradise' exhibition held at the 21st Century Museum of Contemporary Art in Kanazawa, Japan, in 2005. This alternate understanding of the traditional Sen-no Rikyu tea ceremony registers time passing through the room's fabric, as the air-filled translucent membrane structure is animated by changes in air pressure. The colour-change lighting and sound design by Toshio Iwai is intended to represent a garden atmosphere. The entrance opening expands and contracts, obliging the visitor to judge their timing with the movement cycle, as they crawl inside the structure. Once inside, the tearoom continues to change shape, forcing a more intimate relationship between bodies, and between body and architecture. The membrane has a tactile sensation similar to human skin, is soft to the touch, and appears to change by itself as it inflates and deflates, transitioning through several states of flabbiness. These visual and tactile sensations act as reference points for location and orientation, indicating that 'place and position are defined with reference to the apparent immediacy of a lived here-and-now'.[5] The experience of time passing is registered through the visitor's non-passive interaction with space as they take tea. To this extent the inherent dynamics of the project as the membrane transforms enable both individuals and groups to witness a time-based change.

The Temporary and Sometimes Mobile

Gregotti observes that many architectural theorists confirm a Western historical tradition that is based on a definition of 'great architecture' residing near the so-called origin of architecture, one that is 'firmly fixed to the earth and the sky [and] rests on a principle of settlement as it does on its own physical foundation'.[6] It is a generalised argument that valorises a sociological character of time reflexive of an architectural ideology of permanence, conditioned by the physical environment, construction practice and settlement. However, Ronald Knapp, writing on houses and living in China, discusses the difficulty in making generalisations about the ethnonym 'Chinese' as the People's Republic of China has 56 recognised nationalities.[7] The same is true of 'Chinese architecture', since the 'archiculture' of these peoples has led to many distinctive building types. Noting that some have fixed locations, Knapp writes that other dwellings such as tents and boats are 'places of habitation for significant populations who live on the move'.[8] This observation raises the question of tectonic endurance being aligned to land ownership, whereas the mobile and transitory inhabit a different and perhaps more fragile relationship to land-dwelling. Two projects that resist permanent settlement, but offer a different form of mobility to the boat and tent, are Dai Haifei's Egg House (2010) and the Tricycle House designed

Dai Haifei,
Egg House,
Beijing,
2010

above: View of the house showing the sprouting grass seed bags on the exterior and single skylight.

right: The hinged opening reveals the compact sleeping and storage space.

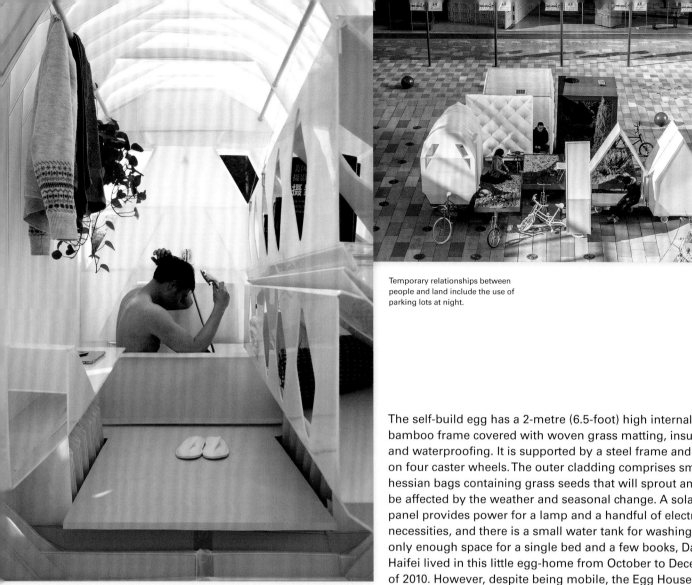

Temporary relationships between people and land include the use of parking lots at night.

People's Architecture Office,
Tricycle House,
Beijing,
2012

The interior includes a sink, stove, bathtub, water tank, and furniture that transforms from bed to dining table, and bench to bench-and-worktop.

by People's Architecture Office (PAO) and People's Industrial Design Office (PIDO) in 2012, both in Beijing. In these projects, formal spatial practice informed by scientific principles gives way to experimentation that negotiates the 'necessity that we live and move in space as bodies in relation to other bodies'.[9]

The Egg House by Beijing architect Dai Haifei is a response to the challenge of building a small temporary accommodation that was inspired by the Egg of the City design competition series organised by Beijing-based Standard Architecture.

The competition explored movable small homes that could also be a place to earn a living for city dwellers struggling to meet the high cost of the rental market. To this extent the mobile unit offers not only an economic alternative to fixed accommodation, but also challenges the necessity for the same environmental outlook all year round – it becomes a registrar of both seasonal change and locational difference.

The self-build egg has a 2-metre (6.5-foot) high internal bamboo frame covered with woven grass matting, insulation and waterproofing. It is supported by a steel frame and rests on four caster wheels. The outer cladding comprises small hessian bags containing grass seeds that will sprout and be affected by the weather and seasonal change. A solar panel provides power for a lamp and a handful of electrical necessities, and there is a small water tank for washing. With only enough space for a single bed and a few books, Dai Haifei lived in this little egg-home from October to December of 2010. However, despite being mobile, the Egg House remained in its original location due to the unavailability of alternative places and the architect's desire not to render the project as a political protest.

This is not so much of an issue for PAO's Tricycle House, which has a much higher degree of mobility. The project was inspired by the 'Get It Louder' contemporary art festival and shown at 'The People's Future' exhibition in Sanlitun Village, Beijing, and like the Egg House addresses the problem of land ownership. At slightly over 3 square metres (32 square feet) in floor area, the polypropylene house includes a sink, stove and bathtub that fold into the front wall, enabling the remaining space to transform from a bed to a dining table, or bench and worktop. The translucent polypropylene plastic enables the interior to register both day (sunlight) and night (streetlight), while the concertina form allows the house to be expanded and connect with other tricycle houses and mobile gardens.

Both projects suggest a future where temporary relationships, particularly between land, people, and building occupation are embraced. The ability to transcend monumentality and permanence is provided through resistance to environmental as well as institutional mechanisms, suggesting that these transitory and time-based projects offer an alternative sociability that is dynamic and fluid.

Limited Time

Among the many projects built in Christchurch, New Zealand, following the cataclysmic earthquakes of 4 September 2010 and 22 February 2011 is the Pallet Pavilion (2012–14) by the non-governmental organisation Gap Filler. The project occupies a temporary public space created on borrowed land that once was a hotel. Designed as a music venue to replace those lost in the quake, it seats 200 people, and during its short lifespan handled over 250 events that also included book signings, teddy bear picnics, pirate parties and outdoor film nights. Because of site limitations (being private land) the pavilion had to be removed within a short timeframe, and needed to be constructed with readily available materials. Rather than fabricate a new product from recycled materials, the project takes existing objects (timber pallets) and explores variability through a seemingly simple component assembly technique of stacking and packing. Three thousand standard blue painted timber pallets were barely altered save for two holes that were used for steel tension rods anchoring the 'walls' to the ground. While using an interlocking stacking technique to make the walls, a number of pallets were displaced enough to support a range of grasses and other plants.

Gap Filler,
Summer Pallet Pavilion,
Christchurch,
New Zealand,
2012–14

right: Temporariness is reinforced through the use of storage boxes as both seating spaces and planting troughs.

below: Lighting is used to illuminate the pavilion and offer a street presence that suggests a different activity occurs in the evening.

Other Christchurch projects also test the nature of time, mobility and the temporary through a range of community-activated projects such as public gardens on former building sites; spontaneous day and night theatre performances; and sociopolitical wall art commenting on the time taken to repair and care for the city. They operate in the space between the earthquake effects and government-rebuilding efforts, such that the overall outcome is a city in transition. This is a reflection of the sheer volume of activities taking place, as much as the emergence of events such as the Festival of Transitional Architecture. They offer a degree of resistance to a devastating event, and it is within that broken and empty city that George Parker and Barnaby Bennet note that 'for a brief moment you revel in the excitement of enforced newness and freedom'.[10]

Aesthetics might transcend purpose in much the same way that the aesthetics of high-tech architecture offered more than its reality.

Shigeru Ban,
Cardboard Cathedral,
Christchurch,
New Zealand,
2012

right: Interior with reinforced paper tubes covered externally with translucent polycarbonate.

above: The lattice window with scaled-up fragments of coloured glass offers the congregation a reminder of the original rose window.

opposite: The reuse of temporary materials is evident from the exterior where shipping containers bridge the divide between inside and out.

Transitioning the Temporary

Although many domestic and commercial buildings were lost as a result of the earthquake, damage to the late 19th-century neo-Gothic Anglican Cathedral in Christchurch's central square was of particular significance to the city. Following the earthquake, Shigeru Ban was invited to design and build a temporary cathedral while the city decided how best to restore the ruins. The Cardboard Cathedral has many elements of Ban's 'emergency architecture', such as paper tubes and a lightweight skin, as well as the ability to adapt to available 'found' items, which in this case are eight shipping containers sourced locally. Arranged around a trapezoidal plan with tapering sidewalls, the geometry enables the ruled surface of the 'A' frame structure to undulate in a manner that is structurally logical yet offers more than the pragmatic. Daylight will fall between the tubes and through the window, providing a continually changing atmosphere that will measure the passing of time.

Conceived as a short-term building, the cathedral is now destined to become a permanent Anglican church for the local community. Although it is not uncommon for short-term architecture to have an extended life, this elegantly engineered building that was designed to be dismantled and redistributed could transition into the monumental. This raises an interesting question about the community's 'longing for permanence', and what might now become 'the aesthetics of the temporary'. That is, aesthetics might transcend purpose in much the same way that the aesthetics of high-tech architecture offered more than its reality. Moreover, with its refined Modernist interior comprising natural materials, the Cardboard Cathedral could also transition into 'timeless architecture'. The irony here is that timeless or classic architecture is conceptualised as the desire to represent oneself beyond the present, and in a sociality sense this recurrent process of time measured from the past through to the present anticipates a predictable future informed by stability.

Time-Based Transformation

While the latter project is being enticed from a temporary 'tent' to a permanent building, other examples discussed above also offer a critical position that challenges ideas of longevity and permanence as a central condition of architecture. We could say that in these projects time is marked by events and activities as much as by weather and land-dwelling. That is, by releasing the architecture from fixed locations, time is controlled through cultural change, which in the Christchurch examples is brought about by an episodic rather than a gradual concept of change, and in the Beijing examples occurs through the dynamics of mobility.

If we return to Gregotti's observation that the West has a 'longing for permanence, which reacts against uncertainty, against continual change, and against the value given to the instantaneous, the immaterial, and the temporary', [11] then questioning this paradigm enables architecture to overcome this stasis. Although Gregotti warns against the open freedom of this model, in that it disrupts and makes continuity difficult, it is perhaps pertinent to note that within this discourse time has vanished in a lived sense and remains only through linear measuring instruments, such as clocks. However, in the examples from the East, the projects are resistant to a fixed location, and as somewhat 'temporary' buildings they respond to time-based transformations where time is local and embedded in the moment. ◹

Notes
1. Edward S Morse, *Japanese Homes and their Surroundings*, Tichnor (Boston, MA), 1886, p 6.
2. Stylianos Dritsas and Kang Shua Yeo, 'Undrawable Architecture: Heritage Buildings and Digital Tectonic', in Brady Peters and Xavier De Kestelier (eds), ◹ *Computation Works: The Building of Algorithmic Thought*, March/April (no 2), 2013, pp 114–17.
3. Bernard Cache, *Earth Moves: The Furnishing of Territories*, MIT Press (Cambridge, MA), 1995, p ix.
4. Vittorio Gregotti, *Inside Architecture*, trans Peter Wong and Francesca Zaccheo, MIT Press (Cambridge, MA), 1996, p 63.
5. Elizabeth Grosz, *Space, Time and Perversion*, Allen & Unwin (St Leonards, NSW), 1995, p 93.
6, Gregotti, *op cit*, p 87.
7. Ronald G Knapp, 'China's Houses, Homes, and Families', in Ronald G Knapp and Kai-Yin Lo (eds), *House Home Family: Living and Being Chinese*, University of Hawaii Press (Honolulu, HI), 2005, p 3.
8. *Ibid*, p 1.
9. Grosz, *op cit*, p 93.
10. George Parker and Barnaby Bennett, 'Introduction', in Barnaby Bennett, Eugenio Boidi and Irene Boles, *Christchurch: The Transitional City Pt IV*, Freerange Press (Wellington, NZ), 2012, p 4.
11. Gregotti, *op cit*, p 64.

Inhabiting Time

In recent architecture, design has prioritised an engagement with time through its creation of temporary and highly flexible structures. There has, however, been less focus on how the design of buildings might impact the experience of time of the people who inhabit them. Here the distinguished author and emeritus professor **Juhani Pallasmaa**, who is renowned for his writings on the phenomenology of architecture, provides a reminder of the importance of what it means to 'dwell in time'.

Architecture is generally understood as a visual and material art form, a spatial framing of human existence and activities. However, we dwell in time as much as in space, and architecture mediates equally our relationship with this mysterious dimension, giving it its human measure. We cannot live in chaos, but we cannot live outside of time either.

Places and duration are integral components of the existential experience itself. We sense the world and ourselves through the horizon defined by our structures – material and mental, built and metaphysical – and this relationship gives the experience of being its very meaning. This mediation turns infinite and shapeless space and endless time into our domicile with its specific qualities and connotations.

CONSCIOUSNESS OF TIME

Our consciousness of time has changed dramatically through history, and this has been reflected in architecture. Experiential time has gradually changed from a motionless or slow presence to a chain of detached moments that disappears at increasing velocity. Along with this experiential acceleration, the practical measuring of time has also changed. In the 16th century the clocks of Nuremberg began to strike every half hour, whereas the development of railway traffic in the early decades of the 19th century introduced minutes as a measure of time in daily life. Today, our personal digital clocks tell the time by the second, and the use of numerical digits instead of revolving hands has eliminated the analogical connection of time with the revolution of the sun; cyclical time has turned into linear time. Remarkably, even the position of our bodies in relation to the passing of time has altered: the ancient Greeks faced the past, and the future emerged from behind them, whereas modern man faces the future and the past disappears behind him.[1]

Instead of dwelling in a continuous duration, we now experience time as fragments that pass us and immediately vanish. The urbanist and philosopher Paul Virilio even makes the thought-provoking argument that speed is the most seminal product of the current phase of industrial culture.[2] This development has given rise to a 'philosophy of speed', as demonstrated by his writings. However, we should not forget that the acceleration of time has been part of the modern consciousness since Filippo Tommaso Marinetti's *Manifesto of Futurism* of 1908: 'The world's magnificence has been enriched by a new beauty: the beauty of speed.'[3]

TIME, SPEED AND MEMORY

These changes in the human experience and understanding of time have taken place quite unnoticed, but they have altered architecture as well as our culture at large. As architecture and cities form a lived existential narrative, architects can especially learn from the lessons of literature. The sociologist Daniel Bell points out that space has taken over time as the central concern of aesthetics: 'Space has become the primary aesthetic problem of mid-twentieth-century culture as the problem of time (in Bergson, Proust and Joyce) was the primary aesthetic problem of the first decades of this century.'[4]

In the classical novels of the 19th century, time is an authoritative, slow and patient presence, whereas somewhat later it speeds up and fragments into isolated images and instances that are reconnected in new ways, as in Cubist visual imagery. The chronological narrative is replaced by an expressive manipulation of the time experience – slowing down, speeding up, halting and reversing. This change also takes place in all other art forms. Along with Cubism and other contemporaneous artistic developments, architecture also adopted the view of the space-time continuum of new physics, as theorised famously by Sigfried Giedion.[5]

This acceleration of time also seems to result in a loss of memory. Milan Kundera makes a rather shocking remark to this effect: 'The degree of slowness is directly proportional to the intensity of memory; the degree of speed is directly proportional to the intensity of forgetting.'[6] Indeed, historical buildings appear to possess a memory of the past, whereas contemporary buildings, especially in the world of business, seem to be all about the moment of 'now'.

NEW DYNAMICS OF SPACE AND TIME

In the early years of the 20th century, progressive artists abandoned the idea of an objectified and static world altogether, as depicted by the perspectival representation and the linear narratives, and entered the dynamic experiential reality of perception and consciousness that constantly fuses reality and dream, actuality and memory, present and future, as Sigmund Freud had suggested. Marcel Proust, the legendary observer of time and memory, claimed: 'As there is a geometry in space, so there is a psychology in time.'[7] The experiential and mental perspective replaced attempts to depict a given and unchanging world.

Postmodern philosophers, such as David Harvey and Fredric Jameson, have identified further changes that have taken place more recently in our perception and understanding of space and time. They point out a curious merging of the two physical dimensions: the temporalisation of space (turning spatial dimensions into temporal experiences and units), and the opposite reversal, spatialisation of time, which has also been elaborated by Virilio. These fusions or reversals are concretised by the fact that nowadays we commonly measure spatial distances through units of time.

In the early years of the 20th century, progressive artists abandoned the idea of an objectified and static world altogether

The electronic era has brought about yet another dramatic phenomenon: the collapse or implosion of the time horizon altogether onto the flat screen of the present. Due to the development of digital technologies, we can now appropriately speak of the simultaneity of the world. In 1992, Harvey wrote about a 'time-space compression': 'I want to suggest that we have been experiencing, these last two decades, an intense phase of time-space compression that has had a disorienting and disruptive impact upon political-economic practice, the balance of class power, as well as upon cultural and social life.'[8] No doubt this compression has continued during the 25 years since his observation, and today's globalised world is increasingly characterised by the condition of placeless simultaneity and an endless now without connection to the past. In this process of time-space compression, time has lost its experiential depth, tactility and plasticity. As a counterpoint to our flattened time, Proust used the notion of a 'chemistry of time' to describe the complex merging of temporal situations,[9] while the experiential time in his novels has been characterised by others as a 'tactile sense of time'.[10]

DISCONTINUOUS TIME

Italo Calvino makes a crucial comment on the loss of the continuity of time:

> Long novels written today are perhaps a contradiction: the dimension of time has been shattered, we cannot live or think except in fragments of time, each of which goes off along its trajectory and immediately disappears. We can re-discover the continuity of time only in the novels of that period when time no longer seemed stopped and did not yet seem to have exploded.[11]

His observation is also valid in architecture, helping us to grasp the paradox that in an era when 'time is money' and the success of business operations relies on timing and speed, we are facing the conflicting situation that while everything is timed, time itself as an experiential and mental dimension is being lost.

Buildings and settings created before the industrial era project a benevolently unhurried time, whereas the architecture of our own time seems to become increasingly rushed and impatient. This neurotic relationship with time is related to the contemporary ideals of agelessness, newness and limitless consumption of our consumerist society. Even architecture is increasingly seen as a consumable product with an economically pre-planned lifetime. This deliberately shortened lifetime also has a direct influence on architecture; the accelerated market hardly has any interest in permanence or the original metaphysical or cosmological motives of building unless they can be turned into a momentary lure of attention, as in the case of Postmodern architecture. Today buildings are increasingly constructed for the purpose of profit, and the obsession with uniqueness and novelty has replaced the quest for existential meaning and cultural continuity. The fundamental architectural perspective of permanence and cultural ideals has been lost.

THE MENTAL MEANING OF TIME AND BEAUTY

The experience of time has a seminal psychological importance as a consequence of our unconscious fear of death. Karsten Harries points out the essential mental reality of time in the art of building: 'Architecture is not only about domesticating space, it is also a deep defence against the terror of time. The language of beauty is essentially the language of timeless reality.'[12] Here the notion of timelessness implies the encounter of idealised permanence, unaffected by the inherent fragility and temporality of life. The longing and quest for beauty is an unconscious attempt to eliminate the reality of vanishing time, erosion, ageing, decay, entropy and death. Jorge Luis Borges makes a strong remark to this effect: 'There is an eternity in beauty.'[13] Beauty is a promise; the experience of beauty evokes the presence of apparently permanent qualities and values – an illusion, no doubt, but mentally an important one.

Architecture articulates our experiences of time as much as of space, though we are often not conscious of it. There are slow and patient spaces as well as hurried ones. Great buildings of the past are museums of a time unaffected by the nervous rush of the contemporary world. We can identify a gradual quickening of time in modern architecture, and a further acceleration of velocity in the Deconstructionist and attention-seeking buildings of today. Our own celebrated buildings often appear to be rushing as if time were just about to disappear altogether. This architectural hurry is expressed in two opposing ways: in the overwhelming number of motives, materials and details on the one hand, and the forced simplicity of buildings intended to impress us through a single simultaneous image on the other.

SLOWING DOWN EXPERIENCE

Every moving encounter with art – ancient, modern or contemporary – slows down and suspends the understanding of time and opens up a view to a calm and tranquil duration. The experience is liberated from the flow of time, and we encounter the work as a duration or permanence rather than a passing impression. 'An artist is worth a thousand centuries,' Paul Valéry appropriately promises.[14]

In the same way that we might encounter the presence of time almost as a still and heavy liquid when reading Anton Chekhov's short story 'The Steppe' (1888), we can experience a slow and dense time when entering a Romanesque cloister or a medieval cathedral, or walking along the streets of an old town. This experience is comforting and healing as it enables us to dwell in the continuum of time as much as in space. In his *In Search of Lost Time* (1871–1922) Proust describes the gradually released time dimension of the Combray Church:

> All this made of the church for me something entirely different from the rest of the town – an edifice occupying, so to speak, a four-dimensional space – the name of the fourth being Time – extending through the centuries its ancient nave, which, bay after bay, chapel after chapel, seemed to stretch across and conquer not merely a few yards of soil – but each successive epoch from which it emerged.[15]

Here, the historicity of the edifice and its parts turns into an archaeology of time as the structure gradually reveals its layered architectural narrative. As such, profound works of architecture and art serve as bridges between eras, connecting the most ancient with the newest.

A distinct slowness and silencing of experience is an essential ingredient of artistic greatness. As Paul Valéry makes Socrates remark in one of his dialogues: 'Did it not seem to you that … time itself surrounded you on all sides?'[16] Yet, we can also experience a similar dense and tactile temporal reality in the master works of modernity. These buildings do not merely communicate the dimension of 'now-ness'; they invite us into a deep timeless space by activating the historical depth dimension. The view that modernity has turned its back on history and time seems a complete misinterpretation. Great works always enter into a dialogue with the past, making us sense time as an authoritative and calming presence and continuum, not a momentary or disappearing instant. The greatest of buildings, such as the Karnak Temple Complex in Luxor (2055 BC–AD 100) eliminate the identification of time as a progression altogether; time is

Karnak Temple Complex,
Luxor,
Egypt,
2055 BC–100 AD

The authoritative and gigantic architectural order fuses the separate dimensions of space, time and matter into a singular existential experience.

Dimitris Pikionis,
Landscaping for the Acropolis,
Athens,
1951-7

The pathways, compiled of fragments
of natural and found man-made stones,
evoke a dense architectural narrative with
a feeling of deep time.

The layering of styles and the
juxtaposition of different uses
and activities – commonplace
and ceremonial, utilitarian
and symbolic – place us
comfortably in the continuum
of lives through centuries.

experienced as a materialised or petrified presence. The masterpieces of Louis Kahn, such as the Kimbell Museum (Fort Worth, Texas, 1972), Salk Institute (La Jolla, California, 1996) and National Assembly in Dhaka, Bangladesh (1974), halt the flow of time equally dramatically.

DEVICES OF TIME IN ARCHITECTURE

Historical settings connect us directly with time and the past: the layering of styles and the juxtaposition of different uses and activities – commonplace and ceremonial, utilitarian and symbolic – place us comfortably in the continuum of lives through centuries. Signs and traces of age, use and wear strengthen this experience: an ancient paved street, polished to a clean shine by centuries of walking; stone steps carved by millions of feet; or a patinated bronze door pull, polished by thousands of hands, turning it into a warm gesture of welcome.

As a consequence of its predominantly formal ideals, the architecture of our time creates settings for the eye that seem to originate in a single moment and give rise to an experience of flattened temporality. Vision places us in the present tense, whereas haptic experiences evoke a temporal continuum. The formal and technical approach of today's architecture has turned against the conditions of the physical world, weather, wear and processes of deterioration, and this arrogant desire for an autonomous and abstracted aesthetic has caused numerous problems. Our Modernist buildings have become vulnerable to the destructive effects and revenge of time and human use, instead of offering positive qualities of vintage and authority of age.

FORM, TACTILITY AND TIME

We desire experiences that mark and measure the course of time and convince us of its availability. Traces of erosion and wear remind us of the ultimate fate of the physical and biological world – Gaston Bachelard's 'horizontal death'[17] – but they also situate us concretely in the flow of time. Time turns into a haptic sensation; duration becomes a perception of the skin. Matter records

time, whereas shape, particularly geometric form, emphasises space and the world of ideas. Geometry and form speak of permanence, whereas materials – through the very laws of nature – trace the passing of time. Modernity has been obsessed with novelty and a perfectionist formal language that do not register this. As deterioration, erosion and entropy are the unavoidable fate of all material constructions, the ideal of perfect and unchanging form is bound to be a momentary illusion, and eventually a false ideal.

WATER, TIME AND ARCHITECTURE

An element that somewhat unexpectedly initiates an experience of time in juxtaposition with architecture is water. Images of water emphasise architectural permanence and concretise the passing of time. The reflective surface of water hides its depth and projects a second, hidden world. The doubled world activates our imagination for the duality of past and future. The life-supporting suggestion of water also contains the mortal images of deluge, drowning and drought. We are suspended between the opposites of birth and death, benevolence and disaster.

To grasp its meaning in art and architecture, one can think of the evocations of water and the extraordinary sense of time, spirituality and melancholy in films such as Andrei Tarkovsky's *Nostalgia* (1983), the gentle and hypnotic slowness of Claude Monet's *Water Lily* paintings, or the architecture of Sigurd Lewerentz, Carlo Scarpa and Lawrence Halprin. Water dripping from the giant seashell into the dark wound in the brick floor of Lewerentz's St Peter's Church (Klippan, Sweden, 1966); the underwater architecture of Scarpa's Brion-Vega Cemetery (San Vito d'Altivole, Italy, 1972); and the reflective surfaces and forcefully rushing water in Luis Barragán's buildings – all evoke a heightened and sensitised experience of duration. The sound of the waterfall at Frank Lloyd Wright's Fallingwater residence in Pennsylvania (1935) creates a dense and sensuous weave of visual, auditive and tactile stimuli. Our sense of reality is comfortingly strengthened and poeticised.

Sigurd Lewerentz,
St Peter's Church,
Klippan,
Sweden,
1966

The dark crack in the
swollen brick floor opens
our consciousness of
another time dimension,
extending to both the past
and the future.

Carlo Scarpa,
Brion-Vega Cemetery,
San Vito d'Altivole,
Italy,
1972

In Scarpa's works, pools of
water suggest a second,
hidden reality, whereas his
narrow strips of running
water seem to advance and
measure time.

CAN WE AGAIN INHABIT TIME?

It seems that we have lost our capacity to dwell in time. Being outside of time is an aspect of the new homelessness of the modern man. Edward Relph writes about the 'placelessness' and alienation arising from an 'existential outsideness',[18] and we are similarly alienated by the absence of time.

However, the magical quality of art arises from its disregard for progressive, causal or linear time; time is encountered as an immobile and deep presence. Art defends our historicity, and its desire is to fuse us again with the world. All great works overcome the abyss of time and speak to us in the present tense, because time as a chronology or causality is meaningless in art. Over the past few decades, uniqueness and novelty have become the prevailing criteria for quality in art, design and architecture. In fact, uniqueness and formal invention have replaced the quest for existential meaning, cultural continuity and emotional impact, and an interest in the significance of tradition is seen as nostalgia or conservatism. Yet, more than ever, we need visions of cultural and experiential rooting that make us again capable of grasping the epic story of culture and our humble role in the making of that great narrative. ∞

NOTES

1. Robert M Pirsig, 'An Author and Father looks Ahead at the Past', *The New York Times Book Review*, 7–8 March 1984.
2. For instance, Paul Virilio, *Katoamisen estetiikka (The Aesthetics of Disappearance)*, Gaudeamus (Tampere), 1994.
3. Quoted in Thom Mayne, 'Statement', in Ligang Qiu (ed), *Peter Pran*, DUT Press (Dalian, China), 2006, p 4.
4. Daniel Bell, *The Cultural Contradictions of Capitalism*, quoted in David Harvey, *The Condition of Postmodernity*, Blackwell (Cambridge, MA and Oxford), 1992, p 201.
5. Sigfried Giedion, *Space, Time and Architecture: The Growth of a New Tradition*, Harvard University Press (Cambridge, MA), 1952, p 376.
6. Milan Kundera, *Slowness*, HarperCollins (New York), 1966, p 39.
7. Marcel Proust, *In Search of Lost Time, Vol 5: The Captive and the Fugitive*, Random House (London), 1996, p 637.
8. David Harvey, *The Condition of Postmodernity*, Blackwell (Cambridge, MA and Oxford), 1992, p 240.
9. Marcel Proust, *In Search of Lost Time, Vol 4: Sodom and Gomorrah*, Random House (London), 1996, p 258.
10. Jean-Claude Carriére, 'Answering the Sphinx', in Umberto Eco *et al*, *Conversations About the End of Time*, Penguin Books (London), 2000, p 95.
11. Italo Calvino, *If On a Winter's Night a Traveller*, Harcourt Brace & Company (San Diego, New York and London), 1981, p 8.
12. Karsten Harries, 'Building and the Terror of Time', *Perspecta, The Yale Architectural Journal*, 19, 1982, pp 59–69.
13. Jorge Luis Borges, *This Craft of Verse*, Harvard University Press (Cambridge, MA and London), 2000, p 115.
14. Paul Valéry, *Dialogues*, Pantheon Books (New York), 1956, p XIII.
15. Marcel Proust, *In Search of Lost Time, Vol 1: Swann's Way*, Random House (London), 1996, p 71.
16. Paul Valéry, *Dialogues*, Pantheon Books (New York), 1956, p 94.
17. Gaston Bachelard, *Water and Dreams: An Essay On the Imagination of Matter*, Pegasus Foundation (Dallas, TX), 1982, p 6.
18. Edward Relph, *Place and Placelessness*, Pion (London), 1986, p 51.

Lawrence Halprin,
Auditorium forecourt plaza,
Ira Keller Foundation,
Portland,
Oregon,
1961

The man-made waterfall provides numerous intimate places for individuals and smaller or larger groups, the constant flow and sound of water stimulating a sensation of comforting duration.

Time as a Medium

Early Work of Enric Miralles

Regarding permanence 'as contrary to existence', Enric Miralles employed architecture as a means of providing people with experiences of the passage of time. Here **Philip Speranza**, Assistant Professor in the School of Architecture and Allied Arts at the University of Oregon and Director of its Barcelona Urban Design Program, describes three early works that Miralles and his partner Carme Pinós undertook in the early 1990s with this preoccupation in mind: the Boarding School in Morella, Castellon, Spain; the pergola walkway for the Paseo Icaria, in Barcelona's Olympic Village; and the Igualada Cemetery in Barcelona.

Enric Miralles
and Carme Pinós,
Igualada Cemetery,
Igualada,
Barcelona,
1995

opposite: Light wells through underground retaining walls allow light and rainwater to enter. Small figurines can be seen in two of the three curved openings to the right.

left: In a covered entry, an oculus directs light across a concrete wall and the floor, changing the space over the course of the day and season.

Architects are taught to resist time. Yet some are willing to embrace it, using materials, spaces, ritual events and opportunities for participation to connect people to changes in their natural and social environment. The early work of architect Enric Miralles illustrates the ways in which architects can 'design with time in mind', for example by creating places for people to hear the sounds of children, see the weather change, join a neighbourhood festival, or observe the decay of wood. 'Permanence is contrary to existence,' explains Miralles.[1] Examination of his early works with Carme Pinós, as well as his drawings and writings, reveals his interest in furnishing people with rich sensual experiences of the passage of time over the course of a day, a single year and many years, offering them possibilities to change their use of space over time and to mark significant events.

Three cases in Spain reveal how Miralles and Pinós used time as a medium: in the Boarding School in Morella in Castellón, Spain (1994); in a pergola walkway for a new main street, Paseo Icaria, in Barcelona's Olympic Village (1992): and in the Igualada Cemetery in Barcelona's industrial peripheral city of Igualada (1995).

The Boarding School in Morella was built carefully into a steep site juxtaposed below the natural rocky landscape and an ancient hilltop castle. Paseo Icaria extends along three of Barcelona's Eixample blocks, and the Igualada project transformed a linear, descending cut of old stone quarry into a new municipal cemetery. Unlike the larger projects that followed, the human scale of these early works allowed the two architects to give up full control of how they would be experienced and, instead, experiment with possibilities of how they could change over time. Now, with the patina of 20 years, we can understand in new ways how architects may embrace time rather than resist it.

Over the Day

'I would like our designs interpreted: as if they were structural prototypes, transparent supports, an architecture that, once built, is full of natural phenomena, from the shadows, air, flowing water,' states Miralles.[2] Each day, sunlight moves across a wall at the Igualada Cemetery. Leaves move, and the shadows they produce shimmer and migrate as the sun changes position across the sky. Similar movements of shadows from trees and the pergola occur at the Paseo Icaria, sheltering people in their daily routines as they cross the wide avenue. At Igualada, rainwater flows through openings, brushing across concrete surfaces in the same way that light grazes the same concrete at other times. In these ways, people experience the passage of time through instruments designed by the architects: carefully positioned openings in concrete, planted trees, wooden planks overhead, and material surfaces that capture shadows.

Spaces are changed through human actions. Opening and closing doors at the Boarding School in Morella mark different times of the day. Each morning, the teachers open the large wood and steel pivot door that connects the entrance lobby with the adjacent event space where children

Enric Miralles and Carme Pinós, Boarding School in Morella, Castellón, Spain, 1994

above: A view through the fog filters the view of the adjacent valley and distant geology. Classrooms and communal spaces offer similar views, framing time-based weather phenomena against the distant background.

right: A wood and steel pivot door (centre left) connects the entrance lobby beyond with an event room where children meet in the morning. A concrete pivot door, with fold-down metal steps and a steel chain as a handrail, is here seen open (centre right), but is normally hidden in the wall of the event room.

wait. This marks the beginning of the school day as much as it changes the space. To reach a storage space, teachers open another pivot door hidden in a wall, and fold down the steel plates that serve as steps, hanging from a metal chain used as a handrail. Other hidden doors surround this changeable event space; some are used every day, some occasionally, and some reportedly never used. Kinetic devices like these that require people to participate to change the space are also present at Igualada in the form of rolling steel crypt doors and moveable entrance gates made of rusting Corten steel.

Many of the classrooms and other spaces at Morella are oriented towards an adjacent eastern valley, providing views through the frequent fog and rain that the city is known for throughout Spain. The open-plan design and the connections between spaces convey the sounds of children across the day. Such design features of orientation, open space and large doors between rooms invite connections to other people within the same building and to the external environment. One experiences the momentary activation of the architecture by people and the environment over time.

Over a Year

Space and vegetation are designed to be experienced over the course of a year through experiences of seasonal change and local rituals. In the Igualada Cemetery, leaves and pine needles accumulate under trees and within the steel and stone gabion walls, creating sensations of being one with the natural world and its cycles. At the Morella school, trees and groundcover immediately outside the entrance spaces and the windows of each classroom allow students and teachers to see the world change by season as they spend time indoors. Teachers report that in the winter students experience the chill of cold hallways as they hurry from classroom to classroom between periods.

At the Paseo Icaria, the series of pergolas was designed to modulate the human scale of the new main street: 'Gradually,' says the architect, 'the avenue ceases being an avenue and instead becomes a series of houses along little patios (courtyards).'[3] This indicates Miralles's intention to transform the broad avenue into a series of human-scaled experiences. Today, people pass along the pedestrian avenue under the shade of the pergolas to the El Centre de la Vila mall for food shopping, dining, movies and other neighbourhood services. A design collage by the architects shows the pergola as a structure for the annual Festa Major, with giant festival saints mounted on top. Though there is so far no record of such an event in Paseo Icaria, those who know the drawings and writings still await this use. At Igualada, small circular openings in the concrete tombs designed by the architects provide a place for visitors to leave flowers on annual occasions such as holidays, saints' days and birthdays.

Enric Miralles
and Carme Pinós,
Igualada Cemetery,
Igualada,
Barcelona,
1995

The accumulation of pine needles, rusting Corten rebar and settling stones visible in the gabion walls. Needles fall each season and aggregate over many years.

Enric Miralles
and Carme Pinós,
Pergola walkway for
the Paseo Icaria,
Olympic Village,
Barcelona,
1992

The pergola, made with steel supports and wood planks, surrounds a tree, creating shade for pedestrians from the intense sun and protection from the passing traffic.

Over Many Years

'I want that my architecture has a quality of living beings, and it doesn't matter that they are imperfect, beautiful or ugly. One finds that each work lives all the imaginable until its definitive disappearance. Only after arriving at its destruction can we think to build it.'[4] This philosophical attitude towards time, understood as extending over years and ending in eventual destruction, is architecturally the most powerful of the three experiences of time illustrated here, and also the most consequential. At the Igualada Cemetery, the position of wood floor timbers cast into the concrete ground has been described as frozen in time.[5] The physical material decay of the same timbers leads to hazardous conditions, forcing the owners to intervene to make repairs, to leave safety cones over hazardous openings, or to completely discontinue its use. Maintenance crews at the cemetery fill open gaps between the timbers with concrete. Timbers with significant decay are removed from the concrete ground and replaced with new ones that can be seen stored in the covered driveway entrance to the cemetery building. Replacing the timbers leaves new concrete adjacent to weathered older concrete – visible traces of the process of resisting time.

Many of the original Corten light fixtures at Igualada have decayed to the point that they have been removed, leaving their triangular bases as fragments of the past. In the concrete, unused or disused openings for tree planters can also still be seen. At the Paseo Icaria, the overhead wood planks of the pergola are replaced to prevent the possibility of them falling on people. Decay and deterioration show the passage of time, but due to safety issues also require careful judgement as to when to mark the final use of the work. The growth of trees and vines at both the Paseo Icaria and Igualada balances the decay of materials as if the architecture works to become one with the site over time: 'It is impressive for a project to be placed in time through its use,' states Miralles, 'when you have a sensation that the thing is working on its own.'[6]

Enric Miralles
and Carme Pinós,
Igualada Cemetery,
Igualada,
Barcelona,
1995

above: Looking back to the entrance of the cemetery, the Corten steel tubes of the entrance gates are visible. In the foreground are wood timbers in various stages of decay, some marked with caution cones. To the left is at least one unused planter opening in the concrete ground plane.

right: Decayed floor timbers and new concrete filling in the timber.

Open to Possibilities

Other design features invite rituals that happen only once. At Igualada, the concrete covers of tombs and adjacent funeral stands, unused and unmarked over 20 years, await the day they will become a final resting place. Since the opening of the cemetery in 1995, dark shadows have filled the empty wall tombs, which have gradually been filled, transforming the voids into an abstract homogeneous surface of white marble covers marked with specific names, years, text and photographic images of the individuals who now rest inside. The entrance gates to the cemetery frequently change, opening and closing, transforming from a low, horizontal position to towers as tall as 3 metres (10 feet). At the Paseo Icaria, each pergola undergoes a progressive transformation along the avenue, from the imagery of an upright tree to one of a horizontal canopy – a metaphor for the future procession of carnival figures and giants, according to Miralles.[7]

At Igualada, varieties of fruit rest in careful rows between the strangely curved stone ridges of a never-used funeral stand, reminiscent of the Jewish tradition of leaving stones on flat memorial surfaces. Miralles's own tomb is located at the cemetery. Sliding the heavy steel door aside reveals a variety of messages from visitors on the light concrete, in different languages, in different handwriting and often dated, *in memoria*. In one message, the open voids in the concrete have been used as points to connect the lines of a drawing. Both the fruit and the drawing, less or more permanent, demonstrate an architecture that invites participation.

It is hard to imagine that any particular architectural feature of the Miralles and Pinós projects here was designed with a particular time or specific human engagement in mind. But it is evident that the pergola walkway, the school and the cemetery, like some of Miralles's smaller furniture designs, await human participation. His wood InesTable (1993) has multiple moving pieces that can be used to create varying forms for different uses. The concrete Lungomare Bench (2000), often seen in public spaces including Barcelona's waterfront, has an undulating surface with undefined seating positions. People often sit upright or recline, or lie down completely, facing the sky. The works do not prescribe a single use, but invite various kinds of participation. They wait for their use to be activated over time. This approach to time and participation is similar to Sou Fujimoto's idea of 'primitive futures',[8] that architecture is designed to allow people to find their unique place over time, rather than creating a prescribed physical form and supported experience that is the same over time. This is a departure from Le Corbusier's Modulor anthropomorphic scale of proportions that supports defined variation more across space than across time.

Open to Eternal Forces

'The solution to getting in touch with time is to not make things that are indestructible,' says Miralles.[9] Though he accepted that some part of any built architecture is destructible, unlike many architects he also recognised that such an unavoidable circumstance offers opportunities to engage the participation of individuals and society. Working with the medium of time means understanding, planning for and awaiting changing external forces of the natural and human environment, and designing different ways for people to experience these. It acknowledges and requires the active participation of everyday visitors as well as society's decisions regarding how and for what length of time the architecture will live. 'I think the greater part of our ideas are not ours. They form parts of a sort of spirit of the times. The spirit of a particular time is shaped more by critical ability, the ability a society has to interpret, than by the forms of architects.'[10] Working with the medium of time requires an awareness of something external acting upon the work – the environment, individuals or the collective society. This kind of awareness does not depend upon particular knowledge of specific experiential changes over the day, year or a lifetime, but rather on a general philosophy that is open to and accepting of a world that changes. ⌂

Notes

1. Anatxu Zabalbeascoa and Javier Rodríguez Marcos, *Miralles Tagliabue: Time Architecture*, Gustavo Gili (Barcelona), 1999, p 58.
2. Benedetta Tagliabue, 'No Es Serio Este Cemeterio', *L'architettura cronache e storia*, 409, November 1989, p 845.
3. Zabalbeascoa and Rodríguez Marcos, *op cit*, p 30.
4. Montserrat Bigas Vidal, Luis Bravo Farré and Gustavo Contepomi, 'Espacio, Tiempo y Perspectiva en la Construccion de la Mirada Arquitectonica Contemporanea: De Hockney a Miralles', *EGA: revista de expresión gráfica arquitectónica*, 15, 2013, p 131.
5. Benedetta Tagliabue (ed), *Enric Miralles: Opere e progetti*, Electa (Milan), 1996.
6. Alejandro Zaera-Polo, 'A Conversation with Enric Miralles', *Enric Miralles: El Croquis*, 72 (II), 1995, p 11.
7. Luis Diego Quiros, Stefanie MaKenzie and Derek McMurray, 'Enric Miralles: Architecture of Time', 2005: www.quirpa.com/docs/architecture_of_time__enric_miralles.html.
8. Sou Fujimoto, *Primitive Future*, Inax Shuppan (Tokyo), 2008.
9. Zabalbeascoa and Rodríguez Marcos, *op cit*, p 57.
10. *Ibid*, p 59.

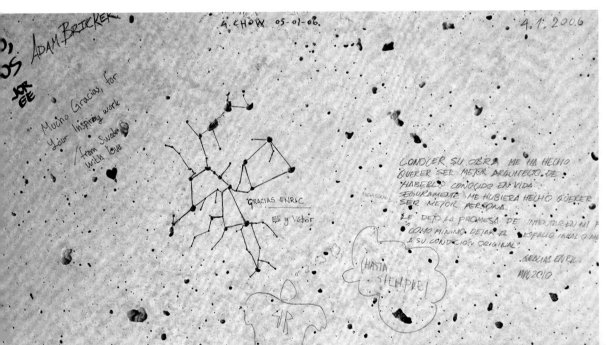

above: A memorial text in remembrance of Enric Miralles located on the wall leading to the family crypt. Pencil lines connect voids in the concrete surface like points in a network diagram.

right: Fruits left on a concrete tomb cover.

Kevin Nute

The Presence of the Weather

Modern architecture has dedicated much of its discourse to crystal-ball gazing – dwelling on the visionary and the speculative. Conversely, **Kevin Nute**, Professor of Architecture at the University of Oregon, puts the case for the present over the future and the past. To enhance experiences of the present, he describes how architects can harness the effects of changing temporal and weather conditions – sun and shadow, wind and rain. Design can heighten the sensory stimuli these conditions generate, keeping us 'in the moment' while still enjoying the comfort of being indoors.

Aritomo Yamagata and Jihei Ogawa, Internal courtyard garden, Murin-an Villa, Kyoto, 1894

Enclosure of weather-generated movement in an internal courtyard designed to seem like part of the surrounding interior space.

While much attention has been given to the past and future in building design, the one temporal domain in which life takes place – the present – has tended to be overlooked. As writers such as Eckhart Tolle and Jon Kabat-Zinn have pointed out, however, most human stress stems from thoughts of past or future events, and staying in the here and now improves our concentration.[1] Yet the 'mindful' approach these authors advocate for remaining present relies on meditative techniques that are not always practical in many everyday situations. This essay explores a potential alternative that is much more readily available: the animation of the weather.[2]

Here But Not Present

Recollection and anticipation are essential to everyday survival, and yet for millennia thinkers from a wide range of contexts have been pointing out the folly of spending most of our lives contemplating the unchangeable past or the uncertain future at the expense of the reality of the present. Indeed, the very existence of the past and future has been questioned since classical times. Aristotle, for example, considered time to be nothing more than a 'succession of nows', and seven centuries later St Augustine described the past and future similarly, as 'mere thoughts'.[3] The modern Israeli philosopher Martin Buber came to much the same conclusion – that the passing moment is all we really have – famously declaring that 'every living situation ... demands ... a reaction that cannot be prepared beforehand ... presence'.[4]

Yet much of the time we are notoriously absent, lost in thoughts of other times or places, and seemingly increasingly so. Mobile devices now allow us to receive live information from almost anywhere on earth, all of the time, but in the process they remove us ever farther from the world immediately around us.

We interact with that world – 'the present' – principally through our bodies. The body is not only our primary means of effecting change in the world but also, conversely, of detecting variations in that environment. In contrast to the past and the future, which are accessible only through thought, it is via the physical senses alone that we are able to engage with the here and now. Sensory stimuli from our surroundings serve to make us aware of where we are, while variations in those stimuli help to keep us in the moment. Perceptible change in our immediate environment, then, is essential to our remaining fully present. As Diane Ackerman explains: 'Our senses crave novelty ... If there's no change ... they doze and register little or nothing ... A constant state – even of excitement – in time becomes tedious, fades into the background, because our senses have evolved to report changes.'[5]

Unfortunately most of us now spend more than 90 per cent of our lives in places that are essentially static – inside buildings. As Judith Heerwagen writes: 'Our indoor environments are largely devoid of sensory change, and deliberately so. Buildings are kept at constant temperatures and ventilation rates, the light from overhead fluorescent lights is the same day in and day out, the furnishings and colors in the environment remain constant.'[6]

There is, however, a freely available source of almost perpetual change immediately outside most buildings – the weather. The elements are both omni- and ever-present, in the sense of being everywhere and in a constant state of flux. Because most of the changes they generate are so familiar, moreover, they are also capable of keeping us alert without being distracting – a key requirement in most work settings.[7]

The only problem is that most buildings are designed to exclude the weather. It is the perceptible change they generate, however, rather than the elements themselves that we need in order to remain present. Transmitting weather-generated change across the envelope of a building, then, could effectively improve the habitability of indoor environments without compromising shelter. Analysis of existing buildings reveals three simple ways of achieving this: enclosure of weather-generated movement in internal courtyards designed to seem continuous with their surrounding interior space; projection of weather-generated movement directly onto interior surfaces; and back projection of weather-generated movement onto translucent external cladding materials.

While our needs for both nature and change in our surroundings have been repeatedly confirmed scientifically over the last half century, there has been little investigation of the effects of natural change on building occupants.[8] In an effort to remedy this, between 2008 and 2012 a series of controlled experiments was conducted in collaboration with psychologists at the University of Oregon, designed to test the potential benefits of weather-generated indoor change. One of the key findings was that wind-animated sunlight is both more calming and less distracting than similar, artificially generated movement.[9] This was consistent with the results of other studies indicating the beneficial effects of contact with nature on human stress and attention, and suggested that weather-generated indoor movement could help to improve both the health and effectiveness of building occupants.[10] The following is a brief survey of how such benefits might be practically accessed using the movements of the three most available elements of the weather: sunlight, wind and rain.

Tadao Ando Architect & Associates,
Chapel of the Wind,
Kobe,
1986

Projection of weather-generated movement directly onto an interior surface.

Kengo Kuma and Associates,
Temple of Baisou-in,
Tokyo,
2003

Back projection of weather-generated movement onto translucent cladding.

Sunlight

There are several ways of bringing the natural migration of sunlight over the earth to the attention of building occupants. One of the simplest is to isolate a distinctively shaped shadow or patch of light on an indoor surface. In order for change to keep us alert, however, it has to be perceptible in real time. The slowest visible movement we can detect is approximately 1 millimetre (0.04 inches) per second and, as the Samrat Yantra – the giant equatorial sundial built in 18th-century Delhi – demonstrates, the projection distance needed to achieve this for a solar shadow is in the region of 15 metres (50 feet).[11] The famous disc of sunlight that travels across the interior of the Pantheon in Rome, for example, is often projected well beyond this distance, meaning that from a few metres away – on the floor, for example – its movement is clearly discernible.

The natural migration of sunlight can also be made more noticeable through differential refraction. As the earth rotates, the various wavelengths of light in a regular solar spectrum move in unison, but as Janet Saad-Cook's 'Sun Drawings' demonstrate, a simple sheet of warped dichroic glass can separate sunlight into differently coloured caustic patterns that move independently of one another. Such movement is still dependent on the slow, smooth rotation of the earth, however, making it relatively difficult to see in real time. Secondary motions generated by the heating effects of sunlight, on the other hand, tend to be both faster and less predictable. Air convection currents generated by the sun's heating of metal or asphalt roof finishes, for example, produce much more obviously moving shadows that can be sun-projected onto indoor surfaces through roof lights or clerestory windows.

Sawai Jai Singh, Samrat Yantra Equatorial Sundial, Delhi, 1724

At a speed of just over 1 millimetre (0.04 inches) per second, the movement of the gnomon shadow along the time-measuring surface is clearly perceptible to those watching from nearby.

Pantheon, Rome, AD 126

At the approximately 26-metre (85-foot) projection distance shown, the disc of sunlight is travelling at roughly 1.5 millimetres (0.06 inches) per second, meaning its movement would be immediately obvious to someone watching from 2 to 3 metres (6 to 10 feet) away.

Janet Saad-Cook, Essentia Exaltata, Eugene, Oregon, 2010

One of Janet-Saad Cook's 'Sun Drawing' instruments and the independently moving coloured caustic patterns it reflects on a nearby wall.

The natural migration of sunlight can also be made more noticeable through differential refraction.

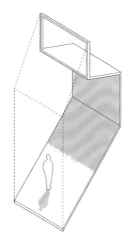

Kevin Nute and Jake Weber, Interior projection of air convection current shadows from a sun-heated roof surface, 2014

Convection shadows are only visible through direction projection.

Wind

From indoors we are often made aware of outdoor air movement through its effects on external surfaces. Of these, foliage is probably the most common, and since familiarity makes perceptible change less distracting, planting can be an especially useful source of wind-generated indoor animation. One of the simplest ways of effectively bringing the movement of outdoor air inside without the moving air itself is to arrange for the sun to project the shadows of wind-animated foliage onto an interior surface. If direct sunlight is not available, placing planting in an internal courtyard made to seem continuous with the surrounding interiors can be equally effective. Alternatively, two layers of a lightweight mesh placed outside a window will reveal even the slightest external air movement in the form of changing moiré patterns. The most effective wind-revealing device of all, however, is probably a simple surface of standing water in an internal courtyard, which can reveal both local and high-altitude air movement as well as reflecting wind-animated sunlight patterns onto interior surfaces.

John Pawson,
Palmgren House,
Drevviken,
Sweden,
2013

Visual continuity between an internal and external room, created by continuing surface finishes through the glazing between the two.

Kevin Nute,
Wind-animated moiré patterns,
Miitaka,
Japan,
2006

Changing moiré patterns created by wind-induced movement of a net curtain outside a fixed insect screen.

Kengo Kuma and Associates,
Water Glass House,
Atami,
Japan,
1984

Ground-level and high-altitude wind revealed in a water-filled veranda as ripples and reflected cloud movement.

From indoors we are often made aware of outdoor air movement through its effects on external surfaces.

Nikken Sekkei,
Mitsui Sumitomo
Building,
Chiba New Town,
Japan,
1994

Wind-animated sunlight
reflected from the
surface of a courtyard
pool.

Rain

Rain is usually considered one of the elements
that buildings have to exclude at all times.
Yet there is a long tradition of rainwater being
actively collected from roofs. The impluvium, the
shallow pool at the centre of the Roman atrium,
for example, did just this in gathering water for
a range of domestic purposes. And even the
gentlest of rainfall can be made noticeable by
funnelling it through narrow roof outlets. Making
the roof surface itself transparent, however, is
probably the most effective means of bringing
the animation of rain to the immediate attention
of those indoors.

Impluvium,
House of the Silver
Wedding,
Pompeii,
c 300 BC

The rain-collecting pool at
the centre of the domestic
Roman atrium.

Eimar Boesjes and
Anita Van Asperdt/
LandCurrent Landscape
Architecture,
Rainwater Residence,
Eugene,
Oregon,
2000

A plunge waterfall created by
funnelling rainwater run-off
from a large roof through a
single corner spout.

Coburn, Sheldon,
Lutes and Amundsen,
Erb Memorial Union
addition,
University of Oregon,
Eugene,
Oregon,
1973

The rain-shedding role of a
pitched roof directly revealed
to those below.

Sustaining the Earth as Well as Ourselves

The natural movements of the sun, wind and rain are compatible with a range of important but underused sustainable building practices, many of which might be more widely employed if they were reconfigured to help sustain building occupants as well as the environment. This would be consistent with Martin Heidegger's argument that human wellbeing does not depend on the health of the planet alone, but also on our actively 'saving' it. Significantly, for Heidegger, the wellbeing of both relied on a reciprocal process of 'making present'. As he explained: 'Mortals dwell in that they save the earth … Saving does not only snatch something from a danger. To save really means to set something free into its own presencing.'[12] For him, such saving affirmed the presence of both the perceived and the perceiver.[13] And since we are predisposed to perceive live change, such variation is also the most direct affirmation of our existence. Heidegger might well have agreed with Marcel Proust's suggestion, then – and the underlying message of this essay – that 'a change in the weather is sufficient to create the world and oneself anew'.[14]

	Sun-Based Change	Wind-Based Change	Rain-Based Change
Daylighting	✓	✓	✓
Shading	✓	✓	✓
Solar Heating	✓	✓	✓
Natural Ventilation	✓	✓	✓
Rainwater Harvesting	✓	✓	✓

Buildings embody our ambivalent relationship with nature. Even as we seek to escape its discomforts by retreating indoors, we remain irresistibly drawn back to it. The built reconciliations with the weather illustrated here stem from the simple realisation that in being primarily a means of intercepting the elements, buildings are also an ideal means of making them, and ourselves, more present. ⌂

'A change in the weather is sufficient to create the world and oneself anew.'

— Marcel Proust

Kevin Nute, Intersections between sustainable practices and weather-generated indoor movement, 2014

Grey ticks indicate combinations in which the indoor animation can successfully coexist with the sustainable practice, but does not draw attention to it. Black ticks indicate combinations in which the indoor animation can help to reveal the sustainable practice.

Notes

1. See Eckhart Tolle, *The Power of Now*, New World Library (Novato, CA), 1999, pp 50–51; Jon Kabat-Zinn, *Coming to Our Senses: Healing Ourselves and the World Through Mindfulness*, Hyperion (New York), 2005; and Kirk Warren Brown and Richard M Ryan, 'The Benefits of Being Present: Mindfulness and its Role in Psychological Well-Being,' *Journal of Personality and Social Psychology*, 84, 2003, pp 822–48.
2. This essay is extracted from the author's book *Vital: Using the Weather to Bring Buildings and Sustainability to Life*, Apple iBookstore, 2014.
3. Aristotle, *Physics*, trans WD Ross, Clarendon Press (Oxford), 1960, Book IV, pp 10–14; and Augustine, *Confessions*, trans FJ Sheed, Hackett Publishing (Indianapolis, IN), 1942, Book II, pp 20, 223.
4. Martin Buber, *Between Man and Man*, Taylor & Francis (London), 2002, p 114.
5. Diane Ackerman, *A Natural History of the Senses*, Vintage Books (New York), 1990, p 305.
6. Judith Heerwagen, 'The Psychological Aspects of Windows and Window Design', *Proceedings of the Twenty-First Annual Conference of the Environmental Design Research Association*, EDRA (Oklahoma City), 1990, p 270.
7. The Kaplans argue that this is the basis of the attention-restoring effects of nature. See Rachel and Stephen Kaplan, *The Experience of Nature: A Psychological Perspective*, Cambridge University Press (Cambridge), 1989, pp 184–93.
8. See, for example, Edward O Wilson, *Biophilia: The Human Bond with Other Species*, Harvard University Press (Cambridge, MA), 1984, and DO Hebb, 'Drives and the CNS (Conceptual Nervous System)', *Psychological Review*, 62, July 1955, pp 243–54.
9. See Kevin Nute et al, 'The Animation of the Weather as a Means of Sustaining Building Occupants and the Natural Environment', *International Journal of Environmental Sustainability*, 1, December 2012, pp 27–40.
10. See, for example, RS Ulrich, 'View Through a Window May Influence Recovery from Surgery', *Science*, 224, 27 April 1984, pp 420–22, and Stephen Kaplan, 'The Restorative Benefits of Nature: Toward an Integrative Framework', *Journal of Environmental Psychology*, 15, 1995, pp 169–82.
11. Under controlled laboratory conditions the slowest speed of movement we are able to see is around 0.6 millimetres (0.02 inches) per second, but for most practical purposes it is closer to 1 millimetre (0.04 inches) per second. The projection distance required to generate a solar shadow or patch of sunlight moving at this speed varies with the distance from the equator, and is approximately 12 divided by the cosine of the latitude, measured in metres.
12. Martin Heidegger, *Poetry, Language, Thought*, trans Albert Hofstadter, Harper Colophon (New York), 1975, p 150.
13. Martin Heidegger, *Being and Time* (1927), trans John Macquarrie and Edward Robinson, Basil Blackwell (London), 1962, pp 383–423. Heidegger may well have been influenced by George Berkeley's thesis that it is perception that brings phenomena into existence. See George Berkeley, *A Treatise Concerning Human Knowledge*, Jeremy Pepyat (Dublin), 1710.
14. Marcel Proust, *In Search of Lost Time, Vol 3: The Guermantes Way*, trans CK Scott Moncrieff, Thomas Seltzer (New York), 1925, p 49.

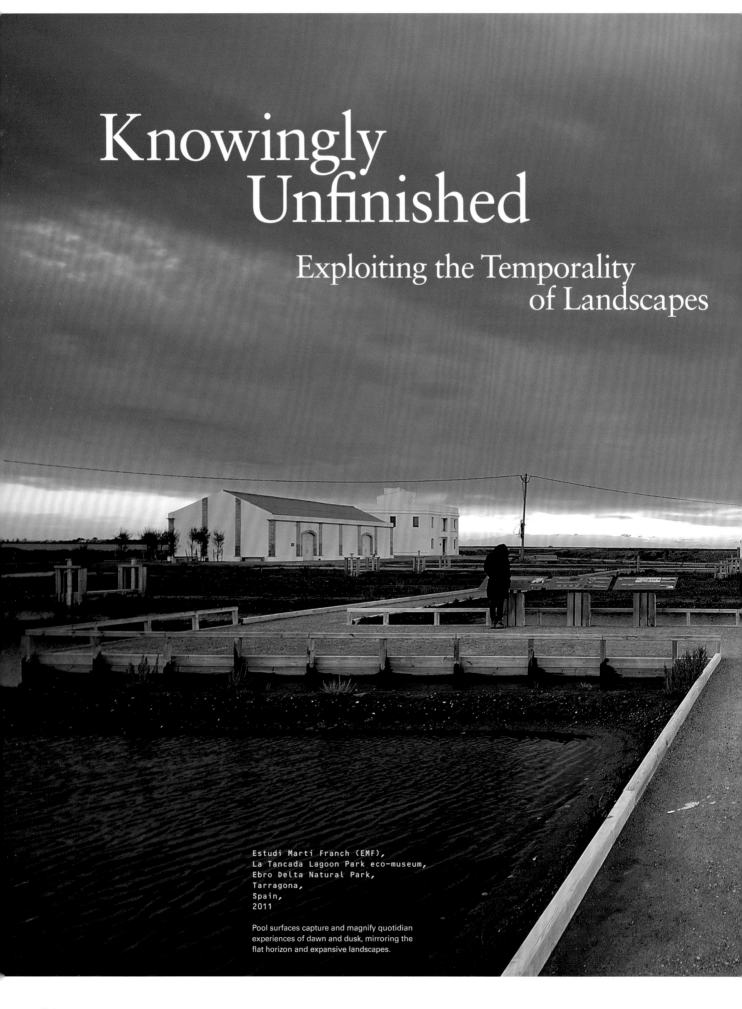

Knowingly Unfinished

Exploiting the Temporality of Landscapes

Estudi Martí Franch (EMF),
La Tancada Lagoon Park eco-museum,
Ebro Delta Natural Park,
Tarragona,
Spain,
2011

Pool surfaces capture and magnify quotidian
experiences of dawn and dusk, mirroring the
flat horizon and expansive landscapes.

For landscape architects, working in a natural growing medium heavily exposed to changing climatic conditions, temporality is a given. Here, **SueAnne Ware**, Head of the School Architecture and the Built Environment at the University of Newcastle, Australia, explains how landscape architects are accentuating this situation by consciously working with the performative aspects of the landscapes they design, as exemplified in three projects in France, Spain and Australia.

By its very nature, landscape's temporal condition is process driven and in a constant state of becoming. Recently, landscape architects have taken the idea of temporality several steps further by creating experiences of change that occur across days, seasons, years and decades, and by experimenting with landscape's performativity over prolonged periods of time. Three projects illustrate these approaches: La Tancada Lagoon Park eco-museum in the Ebro River delta, Spain (Estudi Martí Franch/EMF, 2011), the Grand Parc de Saint-Ouen on the outskirts of Paris (Agence Ter, 2013), and the National Arboretum Canberra, Australia (Taylor Cullity Lethlean/ TCL, 2013.

The projects resonate and connect with the human activities and cultural values of the surrounding landscape. Perhaps more importantly, they are catalysts for agricultural transformation. To achieve this, the designers cross-programmed the everyday spaces of surrounding communities with productive landscapes and employed ecological and agricultural design tactics to encourage an intermingling of land uses. They anticipated and incorporated into the landscape means for losing control of it, trusting that self-organising sytems will advance the projects beyond their own lifetimes. Each engages with Henri Bergson's notion of 'duration' as a design tactic where time is mobile and always incomplete. In 1910, Bergson postulated that 'all existence is in a flux of becoming, moving and growing, a succession of states which never rest where they are … duration is ineffable and is never a complete picture'.[1]

The projects resonate and connect with the human activities and cultural values of the surrounding landscape.

La Tancada Lagoon Park

The 23-hectare (57-acre) La Tancada Lagoon Park eco-museum, designed by landscape architects EMF, is located in the Ebro River delta near Amposta, in Tarragona, at the southern end of Catalonia. The larger river delta and the lagoon itself is bordered to the south by the Mediterranean Sea, to the north by a more natural saltwater lagoon, to the west by freshwater rice fields, and to the east by abandoned saltpans. It is a vast open expanse, always in tidal flux, and sometimes completely underwater. The Ebro River delta is extremely flat and exposed to sun and strong winds, so while it is episodically inundated, the landscape is also dry and harsh. Nevertheless, the particular shifts in surficial groundwater levels enable highly distinctive forms of flora and fauna to flourish and allow for unique agricultural production.

In 1983 the Catalan government's Ministry of Agriculture, Livestock, Fisheries, Food and Natural Environment designated much of the delta basin, including the Tancada Lagoon, a nominated natural area: the Ebro Delta Natural Park. And in 2009 the park's directors, the Institute of Agricultural Research and the Spanish Federal Minister of Agriculture and the Environment commissioned the Tancada Lagoon Park eco-museum.

EMF's project is an adaptive reuse of a former fish farm, transforming it into an indoor/outdoor ecological museum and nature reserve, utilising the fluid but nonetheless constructed landscape. Beyond preserving, interpreting and enhancing the natural peculiarities of the delta, it ambitiously seeks to rethink how visitors experience the wider cultural landscape. The site's landforms are sculpted so that water and natural processes produce an archipelago and tidal saline pools. This group of islands provides vital habitats for visitor amenities and the targeted revegetation of flora and fauna species while also referencing the highly constructed, geometric landscapes of the adjacent agrarian delta.

The archipelago approach is practical for managing the inundation of visitors and water. The first island hosts visitor parking, the next is the reception, the third a set of salt fields and pools, and the fourth includes a restored warehouse for an indoor museum and classroom. The site is bisected by a central access road, which creates a widened central dike. On the southern side lies a single shallow lagoon, adjacent to the sea where existing dikes were retained and re-profiled to create an assemblage of sand flats and islands. On the northern side, a series of deeper ponds for rarer fish populations and dryer salt steppes have been enhanced. On the edges are elevated views from the indoor museum to the existing and new coastal lagoons that feature permanent water plants, isolated nesting islands for terns and waders, and adjacent mudflats and sand flats that become submerged during high tide for feeding flamingos and waders.

The lagoon and island landscape design is quite subtle, in that the site is exceedingly flat and the tidal-pool habitats and salt-production ponds only fluctuate in depth by 20 centimetres (8 inches). The Tancada Lagoon Park eco-museum design encompasses a series of rectangular ponds where water levels are monitored with gates and sluices, and pathways are on top of the elevated dikes. This rhythmic landscape of tidal pools and dike walkways mirrors the larger contextual landscape; however, within the smaller site of the Tancada eco-museum the differing slopes, lagoon depths, salt concentration and tidal inundation create five sophisticated land-water zones, each a transition between distinct plant communities that are fully, partially and intermittently submerged.

The outdoor eco-museum landscape is a new canal network where visitors are guided through a series of gardens. The salt garden, a re-creation of the on-site former salt fields on the central island, is both a distribution point and a transition zone between the indoor museum and reception buildings and the more ecologically focused lagoon pools. Collectively, the design celebrates the site's individual elements – saltpans, intertidal lagoons, flamingos, terns, salt steppes – while simultaneously choreographing the movement of visitors through a reclaimed liquid landscape.

The designers have created conditions for landscape qualities to emerge and for human occupation processes to occur. Through physically reshaping the earth, engaging with the tidal flux and borrowing from existing agricultural practices, they have crafted a landscape that is dynamic yet scripted. The planting regime is self-seeded; the bird habitats evolve, as does the production of salt. The types of plants that flourish in a given area, subjected to the daily and annual tidal flux, storm surges and king tides, reveal the degree of wetness of that location, creating a whole new complex relationship between land, water and time. The constructed ecologies support agricultural land practices of salt and rice production over seasonal change and across successive years. Biodiversity and human occupation change over time, not instantaneously. The liquid landscape is powerfully revealed through unanticipated changes in water colour according to season, salinity, and the amazing reflections of the sky over the course of the day.

The greater context of the
Ebro River Delta near Amposta,
Tarragona,
Spain,
2011

The delta landscape has evolved over several centuries. Arab farmers extracted salt from the intertidal lagoon as early as the 12th century. More recently, from 1989 to 1997, shallow salt pans were excavated for fish and rice farming.

Estudi Marti Franch (EMF),
La Tancada Lagoon Park eco-museum,
Ebro Delta Natural Park,
Tarragona,
Spain,
2011

The eco-museum is a miniature version of the larger landscape, mirroring its complex agricultural and natural landscape systems. The site plan indicates inundation zones, four land archipelagos, and the differing water depths of salt and lagoon pools.

right: Views across the salt-production island and adjacent tidal pools reveal the juxtaposing of the greater delta landscape with the eco-museum park.

below: Section diagrams, keyed into a site elevation photo, designate the subtle re-grading of tidal pools to encourage diversity of plant and animal species as well as variations in salinity.

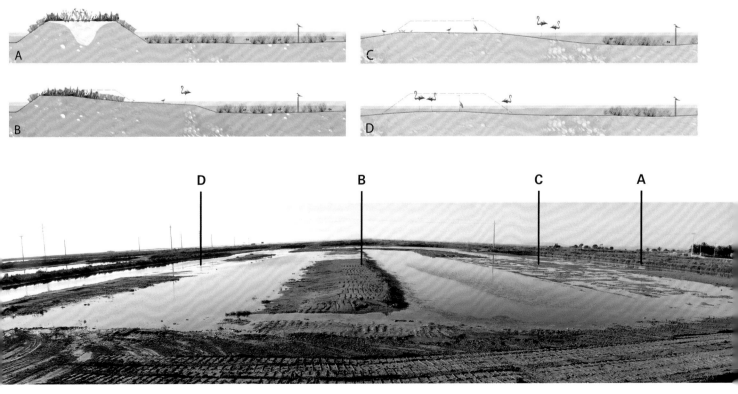

National Arboretum Canberra

Following the bush fires in Canberra in January 2003 and inspired by the vision of architects Walter Burley Griffin and Marion Mahony Griffin for the country's capital city, the Australian Capital Territory (ACT) government published the *Shaping Our Territory: Options and Opportunities for Non-Urban ACT report* (August 2003). The report included a proposal for 'an international arboretum established on a 250 hectares (620 acres) site, six kilometres (four miles) from the centre of Canberra, at the western side of Lake Burley Griffin',[2] and in 2004 the government held an international design competition, which resulted in the selection of the '100 Forests/100 Gardens' entry by Taylor Cullity Lethlean (TCL) and Tonkin Zulaikha Greer (TZG). The competition brief defined 'arboretum' as a living museum where trees, shrubs and herbaceous plants are cultivated for scientific and educational purposes.[3] Enlarging this scope, the arboretum was also envisaged as a recreational facility, a venue for large-scale events and as a high-profile tourism destination. A number of ancillary programmes were also included in the brief: a permanent bonsai exhibition, visitors centre, restaurant and function centre, extensive gardens and an outdoor concert venue.[4]

The TCL design comprises 100 forests, created with the world's threatened, nationally symbolic, and ethno-botanically significant tree species, interspersed with 100 gardens. The concept redefines both public gardens and arboreta, while engaging in complex sustainability, biodiversity and public environmental concerns. On an intimate scale, the 100 forests provide an experience – or rather 100 experiences – of being within and enveloped by mass plantings of single species. At the urban and regional scales, the arboretum significantly increases tree cover and biomass, reducing urban heat island effects, increasing biodiversity, and adding significantly to Australia's national efforts in carbon crediting and sequestration.

Similarly to EMF's Tancada Lagoon Park eco-museum, there is a hybridisation of agricultural techniques, the resulting geometric landscape patterns of which inform human experiences. TCL has woven complexity and indeterminacy through a formal, sculpted landscape with overtly designed forest 'lots'. There is slippage between the landscape programmes, constructed ecology and human occupation; each blurs into the other. The whole combines spatial sensorial experiences with horticultural tests in companion planting techniques, host/conservation strategies, ethno-botanic narratives and forestry trial experiments. The spaces thus continue to be formed, deformed and reformed. For example, in lot 16, the juvenile *Wollemia nobilis* (Wollemi pine) needs shelter from sun and hot winds, so the fast-growing *Acacia dealbata* or *mearnsii* is inter-planted as a protective companion to the pines. This means that the pattern of the landscape and the resulting spatial experience changes over the course of growth of both species. The initial planting strategy creates one spatial experience until the emergent species and maintenance regime shifts once more: after approximately 10 years the acacia will be removed, thus reconfiguring the forest pattern. The process of becoming is carefully planned as much as it is left to chance.

In forest lot 19, only a limited number of seeds of the highly endangered species *Betula pendula ssp fontqueri* (Spanish birch) were available. In order to create an immersive forest experience, TCL's design solution here was the dense planting of a host species, *Betula pendula ssp. pendula* (silver birch), along 1-metre (3-foot) contour intervals at 2-metre (6½-foot) centres, creating a cascading effect as the contours move closer and further apart. A small copse in the centre of the lot is demarcated with the Spanish birch conservation species. After the initial planting, the Spanish birch will be propagated via cuttings, and eventually the conservation

species will replace the host species. Initially, every second host tree will be replaced, then as the trees mature the forest may become entirely Spanish birch or it may remain dotted with silver birch. It is constantly a work in progress.

Throughout the arboretum, landscape and human programmes are blurred as the forests become seed banks for the future, each holding a viable population to preserve vulnerable and endangered species. The 100 forests, Central Valley and various demonstration gardens across the site offer a set of contrasting spatial experiences and activities that complement each other to form a cohesive whole. The conventional notion of arboreta as a collection of single-specimen trees is redefined as a productive landscape of designed and designated forests. Collection, scientific study and landscape amenity become inseparable.

Taylor Cullity Lethlean (TCL),
National Arboretum Canberra,
Canberra,
Australia,
2013

opposite: The overall design of the arboretum is like a patchwork quilt, draped over the rolling hills beyond the Burley Griffin geometries of Canberra.

right: The arboretum is a backdrop and visual terminus for the western axis from the new Parliament House to the suburb of Yarralumla, the end point of the national civic spine. The site's topography informs its planning, layout and planting regimes, with elements that contrast and balance the dramatic landform.

below: During late autumn and winter, the silver birch forest is extraordinary, exemplifying seasonal change and landscape transformation.

Grand Parc de Saint-Ouen

Similar to the National Arboretum Canberra and Tancada Lagoon Park eco-museum, the Grand Parc de Saint-Ouen by Agence Ter also has an educative purpose: that of urban agriculture. The 12-hectare (30-acre) park is located in the northern region of Paris, creating a link between the river Seine and the suburb of Saint-Ouen. The design is an interweaving system of raised terraces and sunken floodable areas. The progression of long programmatic terraces, sloping gently in parallel with the Seine, connects existing neighbourhoods to a new mixed-use development and housing district. Agence Ter have here employed clever tactics in which water-sensitive urban design, and the retention, storage and cleansing of storm water on site as well as from adjacent urban developments, are intertwined with urban cultivation.

French civic landscape traditions often involve intense maintenance regimes in the true sense of public gardens. Unlike most parks where garden maintenance routines are carried out entirely by municipal works crews, at the Grand Parc de Saint-Ouen members of the public, including schoolchildren, residents and various community associations share in these care regimes. Community allotment gardens weave across the site, juxtaposed with green infrastructure, biodiversity meadows, a grassed events terrace, grand allée, playgrounds, skate parks and promenades. Programmes continually overlap, and the usual geometric order of the French civic domain is here messy but striking. Community members and city maintenance teams work the land side by side. The process of transformation is dynamic, both agriculturally and socially. Greenhouse pavilions serve as community learning kitchens, tai chi and yoga studios, as well as plant propagation learning centres. The allotments and greenhouses are places for exchange. Gardening and cooking become the common ground for the nearly 100 different nationalities now living in Saint-Ouen.

Flexibility and adaptation is key to the liveliness of this new eco-docklands landscape. Bioswales separate the terraces, and their depth and location on the site create diverse conditions ranging from wetlands to grasslands, re-establishing the ecology of the Seine. Shifting scales, in addition to the management of all the rainwater of the new housing and commercial precincts, the park acts as an expansion area for when the river floods. It also reclaims and reappropriates the banks of the Seine as the public realm through a new cycle corridor. For over a century these docks were large, isolated industrial estates, making river access impossible. By reviving Saint-Ouen's relationship with the river, the park also becomes a new ecological corridor: vegetative biodiversity thrives in the meadows, along river banks and bioswale areas.

There is a layering of landscape time across the various juxtapositions of space and use: allotment gardens are seasonal and follow harvest cycles; biodiversity plots have ecological progressions; and events scheduling is another calendar altogether. Parts of the park are deliberately not programmed and offer the possibility of enrichment and the evolution of different functions for future needs. It remains an open work where the arrangement of some of its elements is left to the public or to chance.

Time as Change and Duration

The Tancada Lagoon Park eco-museum, National Arboretum Canberra and Grand Parc de Saint-Ouen share a unique status: they are both public landscapes and eco-agricultural museums. They are living laboratories and places where visitors can learn about the landscape and its processes. Their educative programmes make progressions of becoming and change integral to these designed environments. Experiential epistemologies are valued beyond ecological ideals. Agricultural landscapes, shaped and made by human engagement, are deeply respected. The artifice between

Agence Ter,
Grand Parc de Saint-Ouen,
Saint-Ouen,
France,
2013

Meadows and bioswales create complex urban ecosystems while transforming the views from adjacent housing and office complexes.

didactic notions of humans and nature dissolves into something more complex – a richly and densely coded series of ecological systems and relationships. The designers have experimented with various kinds of ecologies, both natural and human, that cannot be fixed, but instead and unavoidably are in constant flux. Each has elements that will change over time, that are neither predictable nor static and may fail.

All of the designers have worked consciously with notions of landscape, cycles of time and duration. The design of the Tancada eco-museum is poetic in its daily acknowledgement of rhythmic tidal fluctuations and the Mediterranean light reflected in its pools at dusk and dawn. Yet it will be decades before it reaches its ecological and agricultural zenith. The National Arboretum Canberra celebrates seasonality, and follows cyclic fluctuations similar to those of the Grand Parc de Saint-Ouen. But the arboretum's duration is one of decades and centuries; each of the 100 tree species grows at its own rate according to site and weather conditions. The design is accepting of trees and their individual senescence, similar in duration to human lifecycles. In terms of agricultural production and annual changes, the Grand Parc de Saint-Ouen is perhaps the fastest-changing landscape. By shaping and managing the land for cultivation and for constructing urban ecologies, this park will also shift profoundly as populations and urban morphologies transform. It will be made and unmade continuously, much like private gardens.

Each of the projects is radical and agile yet understanding of the human need to be within the landscape. They actively celebrate the corporeal spaces of forests, saltpans, mudflats, riparian edges and gardens as sites of inhabitation and distinct ambiance. Their designers recognised and took the risk that their clients and the public would anticipate change and revisit these places to see their transformation over time. The spatial and ecological narratives are implicit in the materials, experiences and processes of the landscape.

All three projects are specifically designed to come into their own well into and beyond our lifetimes. TCL, EMF and Agence Ter offer an enduring approach, not a sexy, readymade landscape for shallow architectural photos and landscape imagery. Projects of this calibre do not employ a consumerist approach to landscape. Nor do they aim to achieve instant gratification. Understanding the value that landscape offers over time, beyond election cycles into generational change, and a willingness to risk popularity by supporting this, demonstrates visionary commitment. Frederick Law Olmsted once wrote about the need for politicians and public officials to become aware that our lifetimes are simply not long enough to understand a landscape's point of view.[5] The Tancanda Lagoon Park eco-musuem, National Arboretum Canberra and Grand Parc de Saint-Ouen, as designed, prove his point. ◫

Notes
1. Henri Bergson, *Time and Free Will: An Essay on the Immediate Data of Consciousness*, trans FL Pogson, Kessinger Publishing Company (Montana), 1910, p 17.
2. ACT Government, *Shaping Our Territory: Canberra International Arboretum and Gardens, Design Competition Brief*, ACT Government (Canberra), September 2004, p 1.
3. *Ibid*, p 3.
4. *Ibid*, p 47.
5. Charles Capen (ed), *The Papers of Frederick Law Olmsted*, Johns Hopkins University Press (Baltimore, MD), 1977, p 52.

The site plan includes land terraces running parallel with the Seine. The drainage and flood control system is juxtaposed with agricultural allotment gardens.

Saint-Ouen has a rich tradition of allotment gardens and apiary production for workers associated with the site's former use as the Thomson-Houston Electric Company. However, much of this was being squeezed out by urban redevelopment. Agence Ter's 12-hectare (30-acre) park accommodates existing residents and new inhabitants of 4,000 recently constructed apartments, which are 40 per cent social housing, making the integration of community programmes and events essential.

Matter Timed

At best, the ageing of materials is regarded as lending a patina to historic buildings. In reality, however, materials often age disgracefully and unevenly, requiring a high level of maintenance and refurbishment. What if materials could be engineered and integrated into buildings not only to enhance but to heal? **Martina Decker**, Assistant Professor in the College of Architecture and Design at the New Jersey Institute of Technology (NJIT), looks at pioneering research that is being undertaken into performative, time-dependent materials.

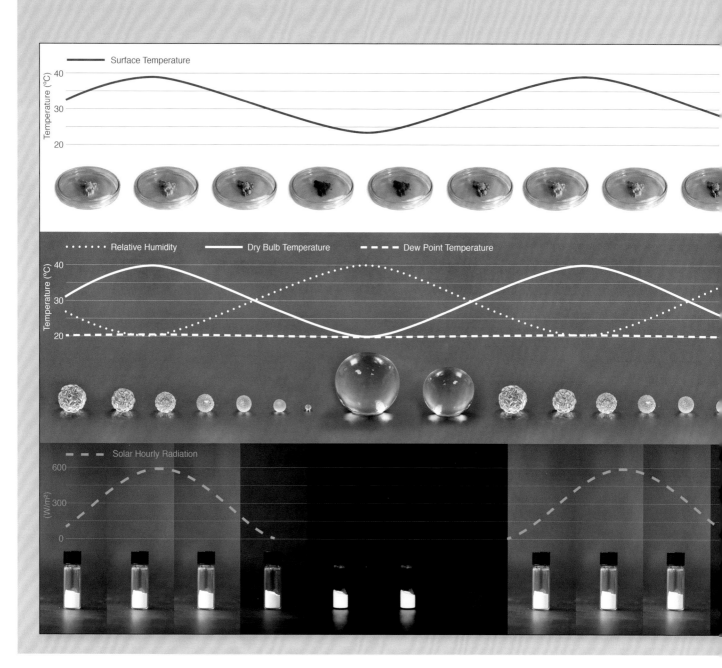

Martina Decker

For centuries static construction materials have served to support a timeless architecture of permanence, ideally unaffected by the passage of time but, in fact, ageing, in response to weather, use and other conditions. In stark contrast, characteristics of newly emerging, performative materials not only embrace environmental conditions, but also make good use of them, anchoring the materials to the same temporal reality we occupy. By integrating materials into architecture that are by design time-dependent, designers can more closely embrace the fourth dimension.

Performative materials are now being invented in various laboratories and research environments where their capabilities are tested in prototypes. The Mediated Matter Group at the Massachusetts Institute of Technology (MIT) has been experimenting with 3D printing processes that produce cement foams that vary in density. The structural properties of the concrete samples can be manipulated with this process at the micro-level.[1] At the Center for Architecture Science and Ecology (CASE), a collaboration between Rensselaer Polytechnic Institute in New York and architects Skidmore, Owings & Merrill, interdisciplinary teams are working on the enhancement of ceramic materials and coatings for architectural applications,[2] including the development of advanced eco-ceramics that respond to local climate conditions.

Advancements in nanotechnology allow for an improved understanding of materials at the level of molecules and even atoms so that material behaviour can be studied at the nanoscale. Materials can then be designed and developed with enhanced structural, acoustical, electrical, optical or chemical properties. These material characteristics can be engineered to vary over time, to be constant or to change in a progressive or cyclical manner in order to be perfectly tailored to particular environmental conditions and distinct design requirements. It is this kind of research that is being conducted in the Material Dynamics Lab at the New Jersey Institute of Technology (NJIT), with undergraduate and graduate students in architecture as well as researchers from various other disciplines.

The materials described in this article are in the early stages of development and testing. Their possible future uses in architecture are evident, but not yet widely realised in their applications for actual buildings. The design of novel substances is a time-consuming process: from discovery to development, property optimisation, systems design and integration, certification, manufacturing and, finally, application. In the construction industry, the development process for emergent materials is even longer, extending until the novel substances achieve wide market acceptance. This can be difficult to attain given the relatively long life of buildings, which does not encourage risk taking in a field that guarantees its products for long periods of time.

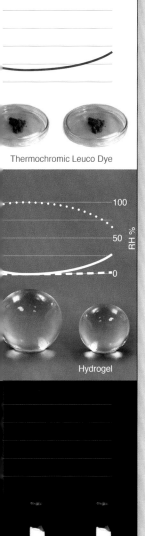

Thermochromic Leuco Dye

Hydrogel

Phosphorescent Zinc Sulphide

Martina Decker, Photographic series showing material responses to diurnal changes, Material Dynamics Lab, College of Architecture and Design, New Jersey Institute of Technology (NJIT), Newark, New Jersey, 2015

Conditions that help us gauge the passage of time, including changing seasons and diurnal cycles, cause ambient energy fluctuations that can trigger a material's performance. Top: Thermochromic leuco dyes respond to temperature fluctuations with a colour change. Centre: Hydrogels absorb hundreds of times their weight in water and slowly release it over time. Bottom: Photoluminescent pigments absorb energy from the sun and re-emit light at night.

Constant Performance

In the past, the durability of static construction materials was most commonly achieved through sheer toughness – a physical fortification of the material level that is ideally untouched by time and unyielding to external stimuli. Today durability can be achieved with very different material means that are actually enabled over time.

Martina Decker,
Photograph of hydrophobic
granulates,
Material Dynamics Lab,
College of Architecture
and Design,
New Jersey Institute
of Technology (NJIT),
Newark,
New Jersey,
2015

right: Hydrophobic substances repel water, which beads up in perfect spheres. The hydrophobic features can be applied to many materials, even sand or granulates, with a simple coating.

Martina Decker,
Rendering of a
superhydrophobic surface,
Material Dynamics Lab,
College of Architecture
and Design,
New Jersey Institute
of Technology (NJIT),
Newark,
New Jersey,
2015

below: Hydrophobic coatings feature contact angles between the water droplet and the material's surface that are greater than 90 degrees, while superhydrophobic surfaces display contact angles greater than 150 degrees.

One excellent example is superhydrophobic substances, where either the chemistry of the material or a particular surface morphology enables solid materials to repel water to great effect.[3] Micro- or nanostructures consisting of periodic cavities, pillars or protrusions force water droplets to bead up into spherical shapes. The benefit of superhydrophobic materials lies in their self-cleaning, anti-corroding and anti-fogging qualities, their resistance to oxidation and their ability to prevent ice adhesion. When materials are bestowed with such qualities, their lives are extended for as long as the intricate microstructures of their surface remain intact to guarantee a constant and continuous performance. Some hydrophobic coatings, such as Diamon-Fusion®, that can be applied to various glass products have been used by architecture firms, including Herzog & de Meuron for their 40 Bond Street apartment building (2007) and by ODA Architecture for their renovation into residential units of the old Tiffany & Co headquarters at 15 Union Square West (2010). Both of these Manhattan projects have facades dominated by glass, and the coatings can significantly reduce cleaning and maintenance costs.

Recently, researchers have managed to develop a superhydrophobic composite that can even heal itself if damage to the intricate surface of the material occurs. The very substance that the surface repels, such as rainwater, can trigger restoration of the damaged surface.[4] This particular type of superhydrophobic material gains its durability from embracing the changing environmental conditions it confronts, using them to activate the healing process.

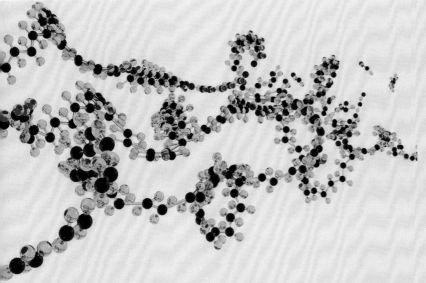

Martina Decker,
Rendering of degrading polymeric chain,
Material Dynamics Lab, College of
Architecture and Design, New Jersey
Institute of Technology (NJIT), Newark,
New Jersey,
2014

Exposure to UV, either through sunlight or high temperatures, triggers a decomposition process in oxo-biodegradable plastics. The long polymer chains that give the material its strength break down into smaller and smaller molecular pieces that react with oxygen to create new compounds that are then consumed by microorganisms.

Progressive Change

In addition to creating active and reactive healing processes to ensure constant behaviour, materials can also be engineered to change in a progressive manner over time. Programmed obsolescence, activated by external stimuli and environmental influences, can be incorporated into the material's design. For example, controlled decay in oxo-biodegradable plastic products enables shopping bags to disintegrate with ease. UV light or high temperatures can cause the material to degrade within two to four months of exposure if the necessary compounds have been incorporated into the plastic.[5] First, the long polymeric chains that are so characteristic of plastics on the molecular scale break down into shorter and shorter pieces. These much smaller building blocks then react with the oxygen that is readily available in the atmosphere to create new compounds that in turn can be consumed by microorganisms. This process of disassemblage and reuse at the molecular scale is planned and built into the material during the design and development phase. Buildings that serve needs of an ephemeral nature, such as temporary pavilions, could benefit from materials that feature such a carefully engineered self-destruct sequence. Materials used to build can then be recycled on that molecular scale to become sustenance for algae, bacteria or fungi.

ODA Architecture and Perkins Eastman Architects,
15 Union Square West,
New York,
2010

Constructed in 1870 with a cast-iron facade to house Tiffany & Co, then encased in white brick in 1953, the building is now encased in glass that reveals the original cast-iron arches, with five new floors housing 36 condominium units. The self-cleaning, hydrophobic coating used on this building can reduce the costs of cleaning and maintaining the vast amounts of glass used in contemporary architecture.

Cyclical Change

Many materials can respond to changing environmental conditions just as the superhydrophobic self-healing surfaces and the oxo-biodegradable plastics do. However, another class of materials, commonly known as smart materials, exhibit the most compelling changes over time. They can respond, repeatedly, in a cyclical manner, to external stimuli such as changes in temperature, light or chemical input, magnetic fields or mechanical stress with a significant change in their properties. In their material response they can luminesce, change shape or volume, take on different colours or produce electric currents, sometimes for millions of cycles.

Dan Beltran,
Michelle Ghanime and
Salma Mahmood,
Soft Barrier prototype,
Material Dynamics Lab,
College of Architecture
and Design,
New Jersey Institute
of Technology (NJIT),
Newark,
New Jersey,
2015

bottom left: With its air pockets in a material composite, this prototype can modulate thermal transfer through building skins. The stretchable pneumatic actuators are individually controlled to inflate or deflate.

bottom right: Another design feature of the Soft Barrier is intended to decrease air velocity at a facade's surface to assist in minimising thermal exchange. The pneumatic elements can change the surface morphology on the exterior of the envelope. The blue thermochromic pigments can change the membrane's colour either to further absorb thermal energy from the sun or to reflect it back into the surroundings.

Thermochromic materials, for instance, display different colours at different temperatures. Leuco dyes can be engineered at the molecular scale to display a dark colour such as black in cold environments and a light colour such as white in warm conditions. The temperature at which the material transitions as well as the desired colour can be adjusted for a particular application. Often incorporated into material composites in the form of pigments, thermochromic leuco dyes are predominantly used as temperature indicators in interior settings. Their currently limited life span, especially in exterior conditions, prevents other possible uses. Eventually one use could be to change the albedo of urban surfaces of roofs, walls, parking lots and sidewalks to alleviate urban heat island effects.

A thermochromic material is used in the Soft Barrier wall system that is currently being developed at the Material Dynamics Lab. In warm seasons the white state of the material simply reflects a significant amount of the visible light spectrum, alleviating solar gain. In colder seasons this material system appears blue and can take advantage of solar energy by absorbing it and then radiating it back into the surroundings. For outdoor applications the material's life span needs to be improved by increasing its resistance to degradation from exposure to

the ultraviolet spectrum. Given the current difficulties posed by climate change, adjustments of substances at the nanoscale that can influence larger systems, such as the temperature of outdoor environments in cities, will be especially beneficial.

Hydrogels are smart materials that can hold up to 500 times their weight in water; they are perfectly positioned to react to fluctuating outdoor conditions. This chemo-responsive polymorphic material can enhance plant health on green roofs even during times of water scarcity and drought.[6] The super-absorbent substance can not only store moisture when it is available, but also release it slowly over time. Material composites that incorporate hydrogels have been tested in active cooling systems for facade applications. After absorbing moisture when it is available, such as dew during the early morning, the hydrogels facilitate a cooling process through evaporation.[7] Integrating elements of materials that control temperature into building skins can support conventional heating, ventilation and air-conditioning systems and hence conserve energy that would otherwise be used to maintain interior conditions.

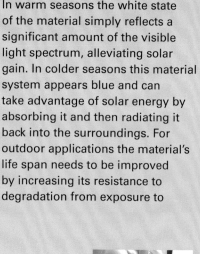

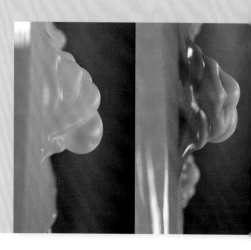

Many smart materials can perform entirely independently of conventional energy production. They can draw from omnipresent ambient energies and stimuli, making them valuable alternatives to centralised power grids. Photovoltaics are the most well-known examples of smart materials that are already widely used. Stimulated by sunlight, they create electric current and offer new avenues towards achieving more sustainable architecture. Energy that would otherwise be lost during transport or conversion is conserved if the photovoltaics are installed at the site where the energy is needed.

Sunlight can also activate the material properties of phosphorescent pigments. These pigments can absorb the sun's energy during the daytime, storing it directly in their molecular structure, and then emit light at night. The Soft Frit project being developed at the Material Dynamics Lab is an architectural shading system that can block sunlight from entering deep into the interior environment. The pneumatic soft robotic structures, which expand and contract to control the percentage of openings, have photoluminescent pigments embedded in their skin. While controlling solar heat gain during the day the material is simultaneously charged by the sun and emits a soft glow at night.

Jorge Cruz, Lauren McLellan, Anthony Morello and Anthony Samaha, Soft Frit prototype, Material Dynamics Lab, College of Architecture and Design, New Jersey Institute of Technology (NJIT), Newark, New Jersey, 2015

above top: To control solar gain, transmitted light and views, the Soft Frit prototype expands and contracts, modulating the transparency of architectural glazing.

above bottom: The photoluminescent pigments in this Soft Frit prototype emit light in dark conditions. When the glowing behaviour is not desired, the thin silicone membrane can be retracted.

Notes
1. Neri Oxman, 'Programming Matter', △ *Material Computation: Higher Integration in Morphogenetic Design*, March/April (no 2), 2012, pp 88–95.
2. CASE, 'Advanced EcoCeramic Envelope Systems (EcoC)': www.case.rpi.edu/page/project.php?pageid=5.
3. Michael Nosonovsky and Bharat Bhushan, 'Hierarchical Roughness Makes Superhydrophobic States Stable', *Microelectronic Engineering*, 84 (3), 2007, pp 382–6.
4. Yang Li, Shanshan Chen, Mengchun Wu and Junqi Sun, 'All Spraying Processes for the Fabrication of Robust, Self-Healing, Superhydrophobic Coatings', *Advanced Materials*, 26 (20), 2014, pp 3344–8.
5. José Maria Rodrigues da Luz *et al*, 'Degradation of Oxo-Biodegradable Plastic by *Pleurotus ostreatus*', *PLoS ONE*, 8 (8), August 2013, pp 1–8.
6. Claire Farrell, Ang XQ and John Rayner, 'Water-retention Additives Increase Plant Available Water in Green Roof Substrates', *Ecological Engineering*, 52, 2013, pp 112–18.
7. Pongtida Santayanon, 'Hydroceramic', 20 September 2014: http://materiability.com/hydroceramic/.
8. Intergovernmental Panel on Climate Change, *Fifth Annual Report: Summary for Policy Makers*, 31 March 2014.

Prepared for Uncertainty

One of the most daunting problems of societal urgency is human-induced climate change. In order to alleviate the negative effects of global climate disruptions, a significant reduction in the excessive reliance on fossil fuels is imperative. Climate change has already started to alter our ecosystems, societies and economies worldwide, and it cannot be reversed with the technologies available to date.[8] Hence it is essential that we not only mitigate the impact on climate, but also construct environments that can adapt to changing weather patterns. Future weather patterns, however, are unpredictable. Weather predictions based on careful observations and temperature records have allowed us to learn from the past, but they have now become unreliable in the light of a changing climate. The many performative materials being developed to adapt to changes and environmental conditions can be resilient in a future marked by uncertainty and a changing climate.

And so 'matter timed' offers adaptive tools and generates a fundamentally new relationship with our environment. Letting go of a preoccupation with permanence, newly created materials can enable us to fully embrace the future and the fourth dimension in our design processes. In resonance with their surroundings, performative materials might enable a seemingly living architecture, nimble to adjust and well prepared for (im)permanence. △

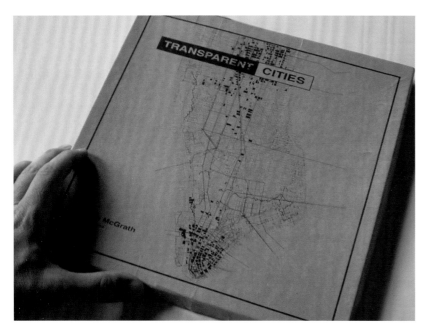
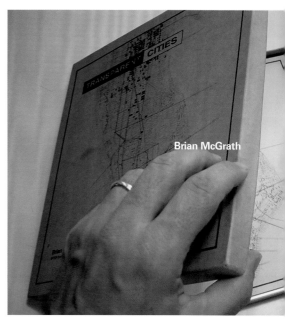

Drawing

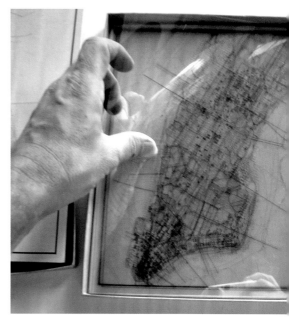

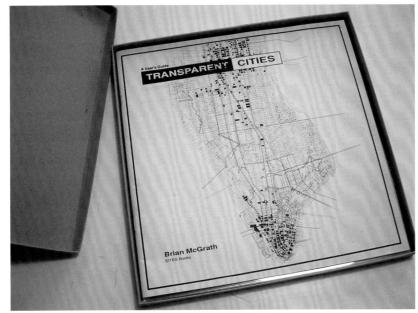

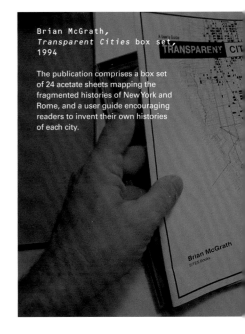

Brian McGrath,
Transparent Cities box set,
1994

The publication comprises a box set
of 24 acetate sheets mapping the
fragmented histories of New York and
Rome, and a user guide encouraging
readers to invent their own histories
of each city.

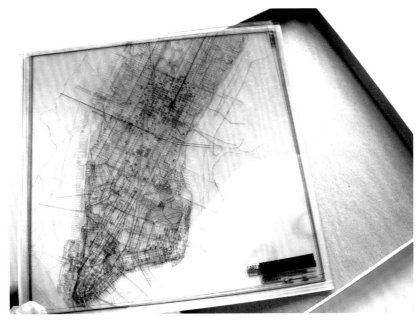

Time

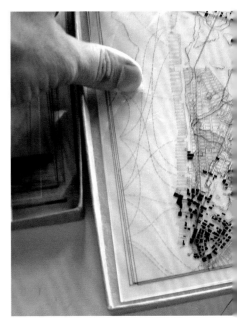

Brian McGrath,
Transparent Cities box set,
1994

Taking place in time, drawing is 'the fundamental act of design'. It is instrumental in formulating duration in terms of process and also the ways in which architectural environments might be experienced. In this article, **Brian McGrath**, Dean of the School of Constructed Environments and Professor of Urban Design at Parsons School of Design in New York, reflects on three decades of experimental graphic work, which take a layered, multidimensional and augmented approach to representation.

The importance today of drawing time in architecture cannot be overstated. Time has become a scarce commodity in our rushed, mediated lives, and architectural representation may aid in revaluing the experiences of duration and being in time. Architectural drawing includes orthographic, axonometric and perspective projection and the new tools of digital modelling and animation. To draw – *disegnare* in Italian; *dessiner* in French – is the fundamental act of design, and its expansion to a wider public through digital media offers various opportunities for drawing an architecture of time. Gilles Deleuze makes a distinction between time in cinema as understood indirectly from movement in space, and as directly experienced in pure optical and sound images.[1] Architectural environments collectively structure an immanent future, within memories and traces of the past, and present in an immersive and embodied experience of the here and now. Drawing time in architecture refers to past time, everyday movement and actions, and the reflective attention that comes when action stops.

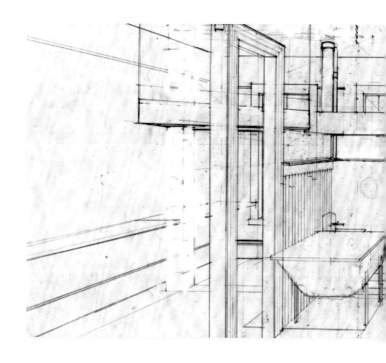

This essay examines three decades of experiments in drawing time that progressively explore architecture not as a stage set for known sets of behaviours, but as producing pure optical and sound images and experiences emerging from deep personal and collective memory. These include hand maps of time as planes of historical construction; three-dimensional computer-generated representations that model time as layers; animations that reposition complex multidimensional information; interfaces that introduce interactivity rather than passive viewing; measured scenes of the micro-moments of daily life; and augmented physical scenes embedded with digital gathering and representation systems. In all of these explorations, the public is engaged as readers and potential co-producers of architectural drawings and co-creators of the built environment.

These examples coincide with the emergence of the personal computer, new modelling and animation software, and the widespread distribution of digital images via the Internet. While technologically enhanced architectural representations of highly realistic rendered walk-through visualisations have become ubiquitous, these images hypnotise the viewer, erase time and mask the embodied and material nature of architectural history, drawing and labour. Drawing time is much more than the spectacular visualisation of movement across space; it can explore how architecture constructs duration in the thickness of being.

Drawing Time as Sheets of the Past

According to the French philosopher Henri Bergson (1859–1941), memory is not stored randomly, but preserved within specific sheets of the past that we search for from peaks of the present.[2] The past occupies regions that must be explored in order for specific events to be remembered. Cultural memory is stored through the collective act of building architecture and the city. Buildings from particular periods form blocks, districts, neighbourhoods and cities as distinct regions of the past. A walk around Lower Manhattan in the 1980s presented fragments of an early federalist period in town houses and squares, remnants of an industrial era of crowded tenement houses, and large swathes of public housing projects from the time of slum clearance programmes, interspersed with hundreds of abandoned structures and vacant lots. *Transparent Cites*, my box set publication of 1994, was inspired by the ruins of an economic restructuring of New York in the 1980s. The project was devised as a way to collectively understand the capitalist city where so much is lost through the process of creative destruction.[3]

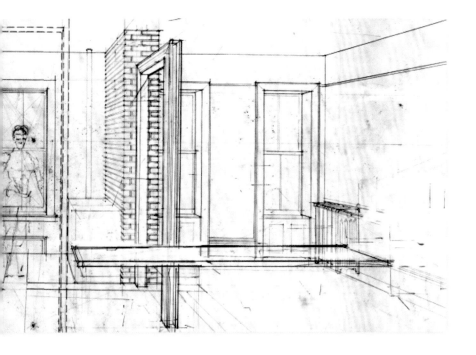

Brian McGrath,
Renovation of East 4th Street,
New York,
1988

Several architectural design-and-build projects from the 1980s explored the social reality of new residents in the post-industrial context of Lower Manhattan. Renovations of 19th-century row houses and tenements provided a way for artists, performers and the new symbolic workers of the creative class to locate themselves within the history of the city.

Informed by my immersion into the troves of historical materials available in libraries, museums and archives, *Transparent Cities* analytically traces the histories of Rome and New York. Various maps were reproduced, all at the same scale, and selected information from different time periods redrawn by hand as separate layers. The drawings were reproduced on acetate plates in order to allow readers themselves to construct multiple images by juxtaposing architectural elements from different eras. The project was a critique of the scenographic, postmodern urbanism of the time, and opened architecture to the more conflictual process and temporal orientation of contemporary participatory urbanism.

Modelling Time for Interactive Drawing

Digital modelling is an ideal medium for collecting and exploring archives of temporal information as it stores three-dimensional form as layers. The act of digital drawing is a time-consuming process of inputting data, requiring the input of measured points and lines in one plane and projecting them in a second and third dimension, while toggling between top, side and front views. The labour of drawing is erased in computer-generated hyper-real renderings. Like the contemporary English artist David Hockney has shown in his critique of photography, normative computer-generated images are like camera snapshots, depicting a single moment frozen in time.[4] In contrast, my Manhattan Timeformations interactive website uses 3D modelling and animation software to communicate the contingent nature of architecture and the laborious process of digital drawing itself. As a publicly funded project, it continues to bring temporal information about Lower Manhattan's skyscraper history to a wide audience via the Internet. The Web interface invites viewers not only to turn various three-dimensional time layers on and off, but to reorient the model from top to side and front views.[5]

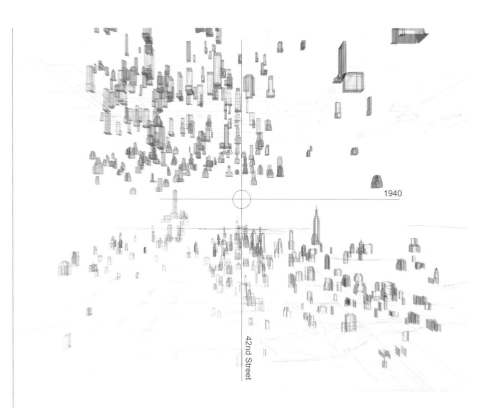

1940

42nd Street

Brian McGrath,
Manhattan Timeformations,
Skyscraper Museum,
New York City,
1999

In the years following the destruction of the World Trade Center, the Manhattan Timeformations interactive website became a memorial as well as an archive of New York's skyline at the end of the 20th century. Reaching a vast unseen audience, this permanent online public art project had a global impact, made possible by digital drawing disseminated via the Internet.

Manhattan Timeformations literally gives time a dimension through 3D software. On the Z-axis of the model, digital reproductions of all the high-rise office buildings in Manhattan are placed on a vertical time plane designating the year of their completion, where one year equals 30 metres (100 feet). The Seagram Building skyscraper built on Park Avenue in the 1950s is placed 600 metres (2,000 feet) above the Rockefeller Center, built in the 1930s on 6th Avenue. A viewer toggles from the towers located within the x–y grid from above, to a view of their position on a vertical time line from a front or side view. The result is an interactive architectural drawing, dense with information that can be turned on and off and viewed from various angles, simulating the act of digital drawing itself. The project resonated with a wide variety of audiences, and its depiction of architecture as a form of ecological succession formed the basis of my long-term collaboration with scientists in the Baltimore Ecosystem Study (BES). As part of the US National Science Foundation's Long Term Ecological Research Network, BES seeks to understand how urban ecosystems change over time.

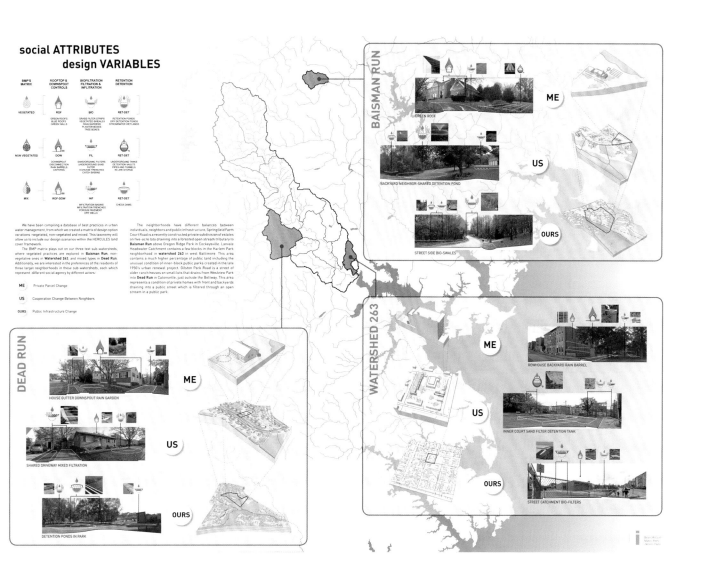

social ATTRIBUTES
design VARIABLES

We have been compiling a database of best practices in urban water management, from which we created a matrix of design option variations -vegetated, non-vegetated and mixed. This taxonomy will allow us to include our design scenarios within the HERCULES land cover framework.

The BMP matrix plays out on our three text sub-watersheds, where vegetated practices are explored in **Baisman Run**, non-vegetative ones in **Watershed 263**, and mixed types in **Dead Run**. Additionally, we are interested in the preferences of the residents of three target neighborhoods in these sub-watersheds, each which represent different social agency by different actors:

ME Private Parcel Change

US Cooperation Change Between Neighbors

OURS Public Infrastructure Change

The neighborhoods have different balances between individuals, neighbors and public infrastructure. Springfield Farm Court Road is a recently constructed private subdivision of estates on five-acre lots draining into a forested open stream tributary to **Baisman Run** above Oregon Ridge Park in Cockeysville. Lanvale Headwater Catchment contains a few blocks in the Harlem Park neighborhood in **watershed 263** in west Baltimore. This area contains a much higher percentage of public land including the unusual condition of inner-block public parks created in the late 1950's urban renewal project. Gilston Park Road is a street of older ranch houses on small lots that drains from Westview Park into **Dead Run** in Catonsville, just outside the Beltway. This area represents a condition of private homes with front and backyards draining into a public street which is filtered through an open stream in a public park.

The project resonated with a wide variety of audiences, and its depiction of architecture as a form of ecological succession formed the basis of my long-term collaboration with scientists in the Baltimore Ecosystem Study (BES). As part of the US National Science Foundation's Long Term Ecological Research Network, BES seeks to understand how urban ecosystems change over time.

Brian McGrath and Mateo Pinto, Baltimore Ecosystem Study, 2010

This Urban Design Working Group, a research unit within the Baltimore Ecosystem Study, collaborates with biophysical and social scientists to develop scenarios of social attributes and design variables for land cover change in order to achieve positive social ecological succession over time.

Installing Drawing in Public Space

From May 2002 to January 2003, my *New York Here and Now*, a digital drawing installation at the Winter Garden overlooking Ground Zero, was part of an exhibition that celebrated the reopening of the World Financial Center, which had been closed since the collapse of the World Trade Center. The installation depicted the physical history of Lower Manhattan, generating new ways of physically interacting with a moving drawing, emphasising the viewer's moving body in relation to the actual excavation of Ground Zero. It suggested the possibility of architects drawing time not as scenographic filmmakers, but as the makers of architectural drawings that move as part of, and within, public space. The moving drawing, displayed horizontally within an elliptical frame, captured moving bodies in its orbit in order to bring public attention and reflection to the reconstruction of the city.

The streets and public spaces around the 9/11 Memorial at Ground Zero in Lower Manhattan have recently reopened. On a sunny day the leaves on the rows of trees rustle gently, the giant fountains gush, and the surrounding glass office buildings reflect the bright sun. The experiences are so close to the visualisations produced as part of the public process of the design competitions for the site that one has the feeling of being inside a computer-rendered animation rather than a physical space here and now. The evidence of life, death, struggle and conflict embedded in the site has been muted by the faithful replication of ideal architectural representations. The spectacular perspectival gaze extends through the power of photography, cinema and digital visualisations, mesmerising and recirculating a known repertoire of clichés. These visualisations were generated as part of a process to persuade and seduce a conflicted public through the spectacle of architectural media, while *New York Here and Now* informed its audience about the histories and possibilities of the site.

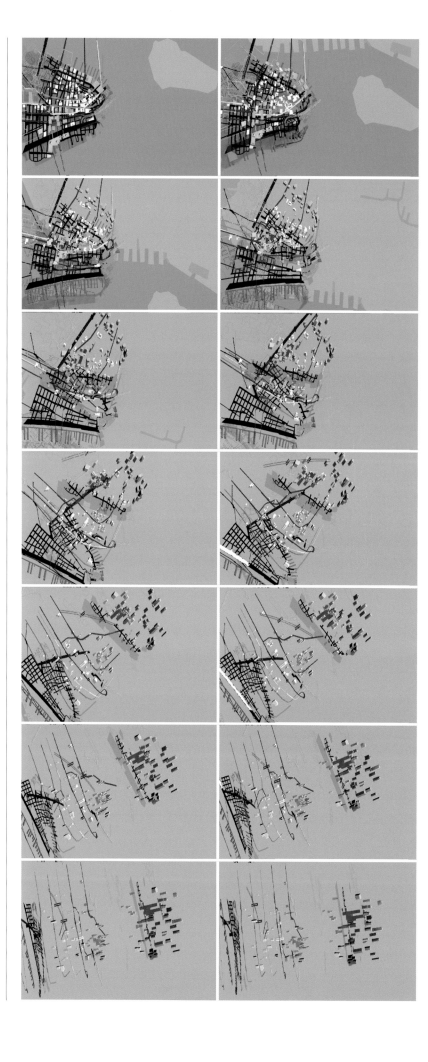

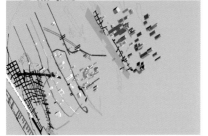

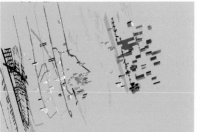

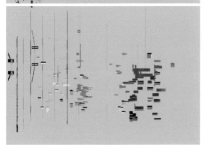

Brian McGrath,
New York Here and Now,
Winter Garden,
World Financial Center,
New York,
2002

In this installation, the layered model appears orthographically in plan as a 300-year chronological time lapse of the history of Lower Manhattan. The animation then tips to a frontal elevation to display a 3D model of all the high-rise office buildings in the Wall Street business district placed on a vertical time line.

The installation depicted the physical history of Lower Manhattan, generating new ways of physically interacting with a moving drawing, emphasising the viewer's moving body in relation to the actual excavation of Ground Zero.

Greenwich Street,
New York,
2015

A view from the recently reopened Greenwich Street looking north from the 9/11 Memorial closely matches public presentation renderings prepared more than a decade earlier. On the left is the Memorial with the One World Trade Center building behind; Three World Trade Center is under construction on the right, with Santiago Calatrava's PATH train terminal beyond.

Enacting Architecture as a Sensory Motor System

The *Cinemetrics* publication (2007) by myself and Jean Gardner includes a time-based drawing system I developed as a critique of the normative spectacle of walk-through computer-generated visualisations.[6] The system employs a second-by-second measurement of the complexity of the movements of the camera and the actors in three short film scenes. Drawings document when the characters perceive, feel, act, reflect and relate in quick cycles in a state of distraction, retracing their steps in the familiar behavioural patterns of life. Cinemetric drawing slows down, stops and takes measure of the movement of bodies in space in order to explore time as a transformative quality in itself. Drawing time in architecture is a break from sensational representations of the mechanical continuity of the known. Drawing time as measured intervals of movement in space produces a way of understanding the newness of each moment of existence that realistic walk-through animations mask.

In numerous workshops around the world, the cinemetric drawing system has been explored performatively in institutional and urban spaces as a way of minutely surveying not just space, but movement and time. It forms a basis for analysing architectural scenes, whether interior or urban. In social theory, the scene provides a way to enhance a cultural analysis of architecture where leisure and consumption have come to dominate modern society.[7] Cinemetrics offers a method for enacting social scenes in relation to architectural and urban space, employing synthetic videography, mapping and diagramming techniques to develop a sense of architecture's potential as a medium for creating an imagined community as well as for constructing new forms of public life.[8]

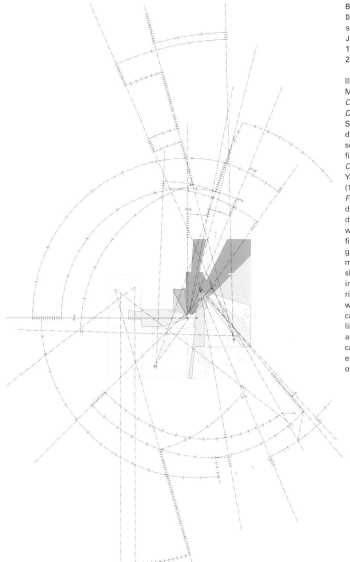

Brian McGrath, Drawing mapping a short scene from Jean-Luc Godard's 1963 film *Contempt*, 2007

Illustration from Brian McGrath and Jean Gardner, *Cinemetrics: Architectural Drawing Today* (John Wiley & Sons, 2007). The book includes drawing sets of three short scenes from three different films: Jean-Luc Godard's *Contempt* (1963) (shown here), Yasujirō Ozu's *Early Spring* (1956) and John Cassavetes's *Faces* (1968). All three scenes depict a married couple in a domestic situation, but each with a radically different filming style and specific gestural routines: the carefully matched montage of still shots of slow-moving actors in Ozu's Tokyo, the Cartesian rigour of Godard's long takes with a panning cinemascope camera depicting his actors like fashion models in Rome, and Cassavetes's handheld camera unable to follow the erratic unpredictable actions of his Los Angeles characters.

Brian McGrath, Jose DeJesus and Hsueh Cheng-Luen, 'Measuring the Sensory Motor City', Parsons School of Design, New York, 2012

For this exhibition, students staged a performance of the same three short sequences from the three films illustrated by Brian McGrath in his and Jean Gardner's *Cinemetrics* book of 2007 – see image above) as a way to survey and draw the human sensory motor system and its breakdown.

Collectively Drawing Public Life

In 2002, my competition proposal, with José Echevarria, for Queens Plaza in New York examined how the act of drawing time can be collectively embraced through engagement with embedded sensors now installed in public space via handheld devices. Mobile smart phones have diverted our attention away from the face-to-face and the physical. Instead, the project explored how new digital tools could enhance public life through the augmentation of physical space and the extension of our senses through digital means. Our proposal for Queens Plaza utilised digital sensing in public urban space, shortly following the terrorist attack on the World Trade Center. It suggested connecting existing digital sensors for security and environmental monitoring in subway stations, on bridge crossings and within traffic lanes, providing data, news and cultural events on electronic display devices.

Today, our smart phones input geolocation data, and we post photos and texts continually. How can this information connect to the data gathered by surveillance cameras and sensing monitors embedded in space? Instead of mapping this data on Google Earth, what if the information is publicly displayed to help us to collectively explore architecture not simply within a spatial context, but within complex temporal social dynamics? Architecture can only regain its ethical position and creative immanence through a deep engagement with drawing time as enacted in public life. An architecture of immanent time creates places for the continual and total process of becoming, producing experiences that push us out of known habits and behaviours and into creative situations, from spectators to actors where established identities are no longer viable, where truth is put into crisis.

Drawing time differs from normative scenographic representation in several ways. It is both descriptive and analytical; it is open-ended, offering possibilities for unanticipated discoveries by others rather than presenting only what is already known or predicted. It recognises time as sheets of the past that can be actively searched in the present moment; it presents architecture as a process of change, not as a frozen moment; it acknowledges space as socially produced and contested as opposed to the idealised purity of architectural renderings; and it actively engages the public as participants, not as passive spectators. Historically, architectural drawing developed slowly as a craft of imaging and projecting three-dimensional space on a two-dimensional surface. This slow craft has accelerated and proliferated through the means of modelling software and online mediation, yet it continues to depict space through rudimentary camera movement instead of exploring the possibilities of drawing time. Releasing the process and production rather than the end products of architectural drawing to a wider public is essential in addressing the self-destructive spectacularisation of architecture outside of time. ⌀

Notes
1. For a more detailed description of how time is understood here, see Gilles Deleuze, *Cinema 2: The Time Image*, trans Hugh Tomlinson, University of Minnesota Press (Minneapolis, MN), 1989.
2. Henri Bergson, *Matter and Memory*, trans NM Paul and WB Palmer, Zone Books (New York), 1990. First published in French in 1896.
3. Brian McGrath, *Transparent Cities*, SITES Books (New York), 1994.
4. David Hockney, *Hockney on Photography: Conversations with Paul Joyce*, Harmony Books (New York), 1988.
5. See www.skyscraper.org/timeformations.
6. Brian McGrath and Jean Gardner, *Cinemetrics: Architectural Drawing Today*, John Wiley & Sons (Chichester), 2007.
7. Daniel Silver, Terry Nichols Clark and Clemente Jesús Navarro Yáñez, 'Scenes: Social Context in an Age of Contingency', *Social Forces*, 88 (5), July 2010, pp 2293-2324.
8. Alan Blum, 'Scenes', *Public*, 22/23, Fall 2001, pp 7–35.

Brian McGrath and José Echevarria, Competition entry for Queens Plaza, New York, 2002

Produced for New York City Department of City Planning and the Van Alen Institute, the proposal links multiple environmental, security and public sensing and surveillance devices to digital displays, public surfaces and landscape responses. For example, the faces of subway passengers and artworks from nearby museums and galleries are randomly projected on an overhead screen; news kiosks glow in a spectral range from red to green in response to the security level coding of the time; and a bamboo garden is watered more intensively the lower the air quality index measured from the entry of the Queensboro Bridge.

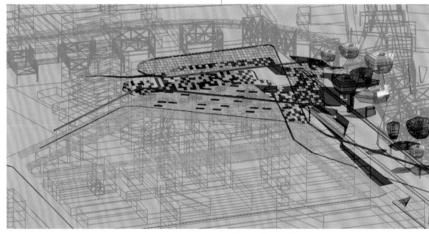

Draw in Time

BanG studio,
Volumetric spirograph tracing,
2014

The continuous black curve traces the sweep
of a point revolving around an enclosed ellipse
that is folded in space. The pink and purple lines
track the normals to the tangents to this curve at
regular intervals. The hue is varied based on the
rate of change to the original drawn black curve.

ing

Processes
of Design and
Fabrication

Drawing embeds time within itself, notating changes in space and duration. For **Babak Bryan and Henry Grosman,** founding partners of BanG studio in Long Island City, New York: 'The drawing is a result of process, but it also describes process.' It is only through this temporal practice that an essential connection is developed between drawing and building. With the widespread adoption of building information modelling (BIM), linear graphic representation finds itself in crisis, challenged by the static inertia of the model. As Bryan and Grosman describe, the well-crafted drawing remains essential to their studio's approach informing the method of 'making and remaking'.

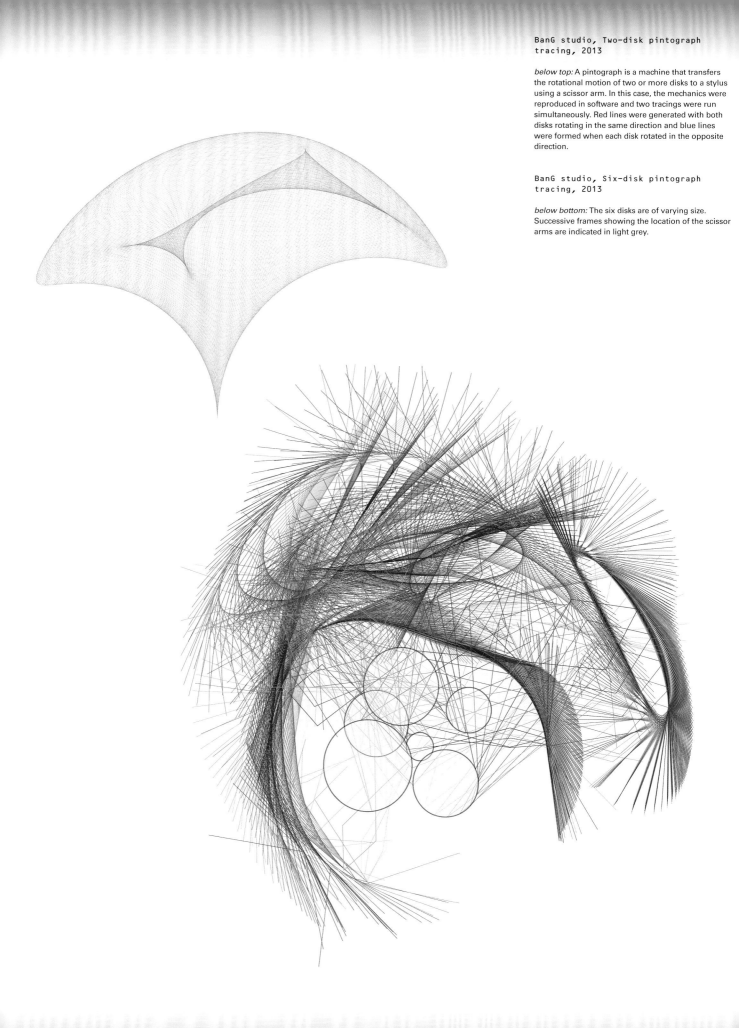

BanG studio, Two-disk pintograph
tracing, 2013

below top: A pintograph is a machine that transfers
the rotational motion of two or more disks to a stylus
using a scissor arm. In this case, the mechanics were
reproduced in software and two tracings were run
simultaneously. Red lines were generated with both
disks rotating in the same direction and blue lines
were formed when each disk rotated in the opposite
direction.

BanG studio, Six-disk pintograph
tracing, 2013

below bottom: The six disks are of varying size.
Successive frames showing the location of the scissor
arms are indicated in light grey.

The act of drawing is fundamental to the discipline of architecture and contemporary practice. However, it is the duty of each generation of practitioners to question the ideas that have been passed down to them. 'Drawing' is as an expansive category that has more to do with time-based processes than distinctions among particular tools, and this is explored here with respect to the temporary pavilion in order to re-establish the critical link between drawing and building that is currently in crisis.

Embedded Time

Time is the engine of process. A parametric equation registers the sweep of the clock moving as a point in space. Time is the input; location is the output. The aggregated output of an infinite series of points – each one a moment in time – is a line or a curve. If one constrains a point to move only along a single vector, one traces a line, whereas the freedom to roam continuously in two or even three dimensions inscribes a curve in space. Each line or curve in a drawing is a trace of both change in space and change in time. The drawing, in this sense, embeds time within itself.

Curves and lines can be described with equations, but they can also be described by the motion of a stylus guided by a tool. A pintograph can be used to trace the rotational motion of, for example, two disks to create a complex path on paper. The resulting figure belongs to the family of Lissajous curves that can be mathematically defined by a parametric time-based sinusoidal function. The curve can be changed by altering the parameters in the equation or by altering the size, speed or position of the disks. The equation and the machine are equivalent. The mathematical and the mechanistic are two different aspects of the same process: a process that turns time into geometry.

The complexity of the curve can be altered by adding more parameters to the equation just as it can be altered by adding more disks to the machine. The motion of the stylus becomes more intricate as it is pulled in more directions, but the resulting curve is always drawn from start to finish along the grain of time. Just as you cannot un-ring a bell, you cannot un-draw a line. Erasing destroys the record, not the act. Time moves only forward.

Equations, scripts and algorithms are all notations for time-based processes. Each can be understood as an abstract machine for producing geometry. Consider the spirograph. The mathematics is complex, but the underlying control process is based on a simple set of draughting techniques that are reproduced using parametric design software. The draughting process is automated by the computer, but it is not instantaneous; it still plays out in time. Each change to the armature guiding the stylus plays out at processor speed, embedding time at a furious pace.

Drawing

Lines are the currency of architectural drawing. A tool guides a stylus across the page in deliberate and measured fashion. Each line carries within it the embedded time of its own draughting. Most drawings contain many lines. They describe the boundaries, shapes, assemblies and functions of architecture. These lines are not created simultaneously; the sequence of their making is, itself, another form of embedded time in the act of drawing.

The drawing is a document of its own genesis. Each new line changes the lines that came before it, and will be changed by the lines that come after. Lines register change in the drawing like rings in a tree. New layers of content aggregate, and are themselves changed by subsequent markings. Time is registered both in the reading of the line and the reading of the drawing as a whole.

Inside the silicon world of the computer, the line is even less prone to ossify into stasis. It exists in a permanent state of flux. While the ink line holds its ground in an ever-changing context, the digital line can morph, twist, bend, fold and react to the proliferation of changes surrounding it. The true power of the digital line is that it can evolve. The ink line, once drawn, does not change; new lines on the page change the context in which it is read, but the line itself remains fixed. The digital line, on the other hand, is infinitely mutable. Its underlying parameters may always be changed in response to changing conditions. Thus, the act of drawing in the digital realm takes on even more power as a repository of change and thus of time.

The software that enables such radical mutability of the line is often characterised as 'digital modelling software'. These programs, with their parametric controls and visual scripting environments, are traditionally understood by their relationship to the architectural model rather than to drawing. At best this association is false, and at worst it leads to an unfortunate and impoverished understanding of such programs as design tools. Modelling by definition is the construction of a single static set of formalised relationships, whereas drawing allows for its author to interrogate and explore the temporal processes underlying these relationships. Drawings are explorations of time; models are explorations of space. The digital model as traditionally understood has no advantage over the physical model except for expediency. The digital drawing, on the other hand, creates new opportunities.

In the conventional building information modelling (BIM) narrative, the model is given primacy and purpose by its ability to embed 'information'. The BIM model, however, is merely a vessel: static and inert while the drawing is alive. Each mark drips with time, exhibiting a complex constellation of part-to-part relationships in which it exists only in ecological relationships to the others. Parametric design and scripting software have the power to heighten and intensify these relationships, which develop and change over time, by expanding the means and methods for making new marks beyond the simple stylus and straightedge. This power is realised only when scripted with time in mind.

The difference between model and drawing lies precisely in the power of drawing to embed time. It is for this reason that we understand our use of parametric software as a drawing practice, not a modelling practice.[1] The embedded time of the drawing is important for two reasons. Firstly, it serves as a record of the drawing's own making, a genetic code embedded on the page. Secondly, it gives the drawing a power to describe processes that are external to it. Through the act of drawing one describes motion,

The six sketches on the bottom
test different sets of drawing
processes for a proposed
pavilion design. The nine
sketches to the right test a
single drawing process by
varying the input parameters
and rerunning the system.

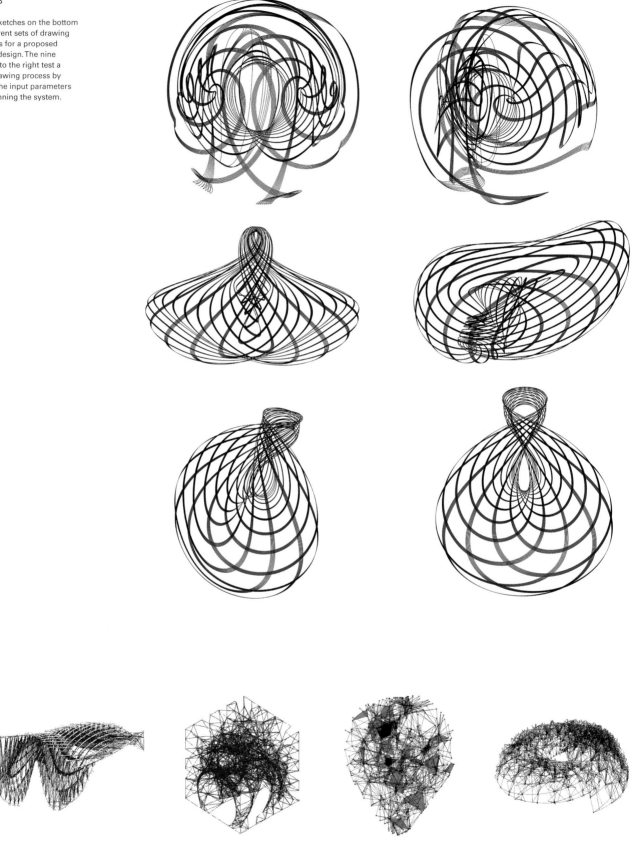

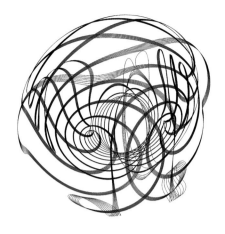

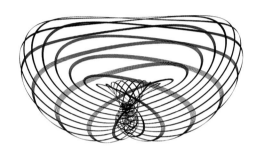

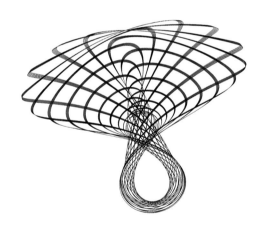

sequence and change that can be made to have resonance and reverberation in the physical world. The drawing is a result of process, but it also describes process. It is generated in time through a layering of time-based mechanisms, but it can be read in an instant. It collapses multifarious layers of embedded time onto the space of the page.

Fabrication

Architectural drawing, as we know it today, has its origins in the Renaissance. Before then, the model was the primary means by which design intent was conveyed from the master builder to the workers doing the heavy lifting. The advent of drawing marks the beginning of the professionalisation of the practice of architecture, and the split between the designer and the executor of construction.

Recently, some have spoken of the split between architect and builder as a loss of control. They have advocated for a return to the model (specifically the building information model) as a means to regain control of the construction process.[2] But cutting drawing out of the picture is a mistake. The model, as we understand it, can only capture the static. It describes form, structure, space and tectonic relationships. The advent of BIM allows the model to speak more eloquently of these things, but it does not enhance the fundamental rhetorical inadequacies of the medium.

The BIM narrative proposes that the model be used as the primary vehicle to represent the design by conveying information to the fabricator. The assumption embedded in this proposition is that the 'project' exists apart from its representation and that the model is only a means to an end, namely the realisation of the project. But this is not why we draw. We draw to understand the project. We draw to develop the project. The process of drawing is a part of the thinking of the project just as much as the making of the project. The model is only a representation; the drawing is analysis. The drawing is a process.

Construction is a process too, and like drawing it exists in time. Also like drawing, it is the confluence of multiple overlapping and intertwining timelines. The activities of fabricating components, assembly, logistics and coordination wrap around one another on site. These processes must change and adapt to field conditions as they arise. Each new mark on the site affects what came before and sets the stage for what will come next.

The words 'building' and 'fabrication' are not used interchangeably. Building refers more explicitly to the end result – a building or structure that one can inhabit and use. Fabrication speaks more specifically about process; the word contains within it the notion of 'fabric' – a complex interweaving of many lines into a coherent yet dynamic whole. However, there is an explicit link between drawing and fabricating. Drawing does not merely describe the finished product; it describes the processes by which it is to be made. Drawing methods are often proxies for fabrication methods. They are iterative and mutable. They incorporate chance and determinism. They propose strategies for adapting to site conditions, and they describe the qualities of form, space and affect of the project.

BanG studio has designed and fabricated a series of small, temporary pavilions to test the link between drawing and building. The pavilion is an ideal laboratory for this type of exploration for several reasons. Firstly, it is small. The size of the structure affords the opportunity to execute the project from start to finish in the

BanG studio,
Jacob's Ladder,
Congregation
Beth Elohim,
Brooklyn,
New York,
2012

The design for this pavilion for a historic building in Brooklyn, as in much of the studio's other work, began in McNeel Grasshopper®. However, it was not until the building of the full-scale prototypes began that the assembly logics could be fully tested. Throughout the construction process, field conditions change how the project plays out in ways that are not always predictable.

BanG studio,
Caterpillar,
2013

Rendering of a proposed pavilion for a London park. The distribution of tensile forces through the system creates complex relationships between the disparate materials.

opposite: Detailed mock-up of the Caterpillar pavilion demonstrating that the physical forces within the material respond differently than was initially anticipated. However, this realisation only confirmed the design agenda.

studio space. The small scale of the building also means that ideas and techniques can be tested at one-to-one scale with a minimal amount of machinery. Secondly, the pavilion is fast. From start to finish the turnaround is short, moving from drawing to prototyping to fabrication and assembly with astonishing speed. Thirdly, the pavilion is cheap. Ideas are proposed, tested and deployed with such speed because the stakes are low. The materials are inexpensive so the only premium is time. And finally, the pavilion is temporary. The structures have a finite duration, which means that the full lifecycle of the project is subject to scrutiny. Demolition, deconstruction and decommissioning all become part of the process.

Jacob's Ladder (2012) is a good example of BanG studio's installation work. When the client commissioned this pavilion, an intervention in their historic building in Brooklyn, they specified only the project title, that there would be five weeks to build it, and a tiny budget. In the book of Genesis, Jacob has a dream where he sees angels ascending and descending a ladder. BanG studio imagined the angels as Marcel Duchamp would have dreamed them: their motion, collapsed in time and registered in sequence. The ladder in the studio's design was thus freed to move in three dimensions rather than extending merely straight up and down. Software was used for the initial formal investigations, developing a technique to control five separate series of lines and to trace them through a series of spatial manoeuvres. From the digital models, the process moved quickly to small physical models and full-scale prototypes. The lines became long cardboard tubes. The prototypes necessitated changes to the ways the tubes were interwoven in order to make the system self-supporting and structurally determinate. And to adapt to the physical and structural realities, the drawing technique changed. This change filtered back into the software model to produce new drawings that became the basis of further physical prototypes and eventually the final installation.

Jacob's Ladder can be understood in terms of the drawing process. In each design iteration, a series of lines was drawn in space either in the virtual realm of the computer or in the physical realm of the workshop. Each new line changed the drawing, providing a new context for the lines that came before, but the lines themselves remained resolutely static. In this sense, the project was very much like an ink drawing.

In later projects, such as Caterpillar (2013), a proposed pavilion for a London park, BanG studio sought to challenge the stasis of the ink line and to find a physical analogue for the mutable digital line. The rendering shown here is a final static configuration of the project, but the photograph of the prototype exposes the way the system performs. Like Jacob's Ladder, Caterpillar was made with a series of lines that weave through one another in space. However, here the lines were not rigid tubes, but rather flexible PVC pipes and acrylic rope. Each new line in the project changed the others as the tensile forces redistributed themselves through the system. The capacity of new lines to have a physical effect not just on the system as a whole, but also on individual lines that preceded them in time, is characteristic of a complex dynamic drawing technique that is at the heart of BanG studio's current practice.

When lines morph and change, as they did in Caterpillar, drawings can very quickly become complicated. It is therefore incumbent on the designer to calibrate the processes carefully. One can achieve a great deal of complexity by carefully coordinating a few simple operations.

BanG studio,
Sprouts,
New York City,
2014

right: Rendering of a proposed
pavilion for a sculpture park
showing the 3D weave. The
shimmering washers punctuate
and pull the strings that weave
between the PVC pipes.

opposite: Drawing showing
the colonisation of the Sprouts
pavilion structure with vines.

BanG studio,
Billion Oyster Pavilion,
FIGMENT City of Dreams,
Governors Island,
New York,
summer 2015

above: Detail of the final pavilion.

right: The final pavilion as installed
at the FIGMENT summer arts festival
prior to its decommissioning and
repurposing as an oyster habitat.

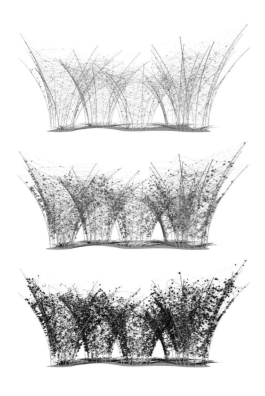

Collapsed Time

The pavilion is BanG studio's laboratory for experiment because it is understood as a physical manifestation of drawing; that is to say, a time-based dynamic process. Both the drawing and thus the pavilion embody embedded time. But how are these layers of line and process, this embedded time, received by the visitor?

The pavilion is a drawing not only because it is made by a drawing process, but also because it is experienced in the same way one experiences a drawing – all at once. Because of its size, simplicity and lack of programme, the pavilion can be absorbed in an instant. Consider Sprouts (2014), BanG studio's pavilion for a sculpture park in New York City. Its structure, like Caterpillar, was drawn with PVC pipe and rope; however, an additional process plays out over a protracted period of time. The PVC is filled with soil and seeds. As the season progresses, the rope is colonised by vines – a third line in the system. In this sense, the drawing of Sprouts took months, but the project exists in the fullness of its embedded time at every moment for the visitor. The visitor experiences the confluence of multiple timelines played out in the pavilion. These unfolding temporal processes (the drawing of the structure and its colonisation by vines) remain at work, but would always be experienced in an instant.

The Billion Oyster Pavilion (2015), built for the FIGMENT City of Dreams summer arts festival, is explicit in the contemplation of its own demise. Each component of the project was reused by a not-for-profit organisation to create an oyster habitat in New York City's waterways. The lightweight nylon rope that weaved through the canopy has now been unwoven and coiled to be used again. The network of steel triangles has been detached and reconnected differently to form cages that are now filled with old oyster shells. The shells, like the concrete blocks at the base of the pavilion, have been covered with oyster spat and dropped into the harbour to form the backbone of a new oyster reef. This performance – the process of decommissioning – is as embedded in the project as is its making. It is BanG studio's intention that visitors will experience the pavilion as a moment in time trapped precisely between its making and its unmaking, and that this moment will be beautiful.

The power of the drawing (and thus the pavilion) is that one can enter in a moment and find oneself caught in the middle of a tangle. The well-crafted drawing reveals to both its authors and its observers the mechanisms of its making and remaking. It is not just legible, but also profoundly meaningful. Its reading takes place in the blink of an eye, but its drawing will always take place over time. ᴆ

Notes
1. Babak Bryan and Henry Grosman, 'Drawing with Machines: Analog Practices in the Digital Realm', *International Journal of Interior Architecture + Spatial Design*, 3, 2014, pp 20–29.
2. Samantha Topol, 'Modern Day Master Builders', *Architects Newspaper*, 11 December 2006: http://archpaper.com/news/articles.asp?id=079#.VZxFE_IVhBc.

Architecture Takes Time

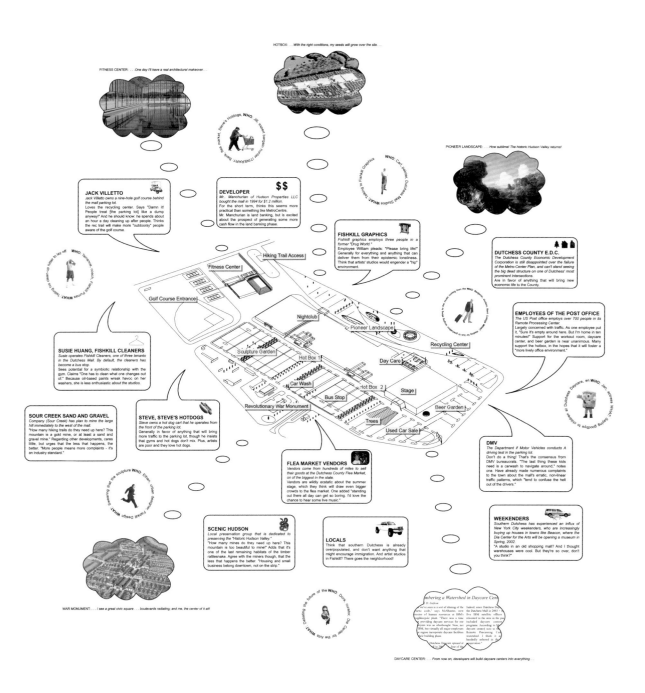

FITNESS CENTER: . . . One day I'll have a real architectural makeover. . .

HOTBOX: . . . With the right conditions, my seeds will grow over the site. . .

PIONEER LANDSCAPE: . . . How sublime! The historic Hudson Valley returns!

JACK VILLETTO
Jack Villetto owns a nine-hole golf course behind the mall parking lot.
Loves the recycling center. Says "Damn it! People treat [the parking lot] like a dump anyway!" And he should know: he spends about an hour a day cleaning up after people. Thinks the rec trail will make more "outdoorsy" people aware of the golf course.

DEVELOPER **$$**
Mr. Manchurian of Hudson Properties LLC bought the mall in 1994 for $1.2 million.
For the short term, thinks this seems more practical than something like MetroCentre.
Mr. Manchurian is land banking, but is excited about the prospect of generating some more cash flow in the land banking phase.

FISHKILL GRAPHICS
Fishkill graphics employs three people in a former "Drug World."
Employee William pleads: "Please bring life!" Generally for everything and anything that can deliver them from their epistemic loneliness. Think that artists' studios would engender a "hip" environment.

DUTCHESS COUNTY E.D.C.
The Dutchess County Economic Development Corporation is still disappointed over the failure of the Metro-Center Plan, and can't stand seeing the big dead structure on one of Dutchess' most prominent intersections.
Are in favor of anything that will bring new economic life to the County.

EMPLOYEES OF THE POST OFFICE
The US Post office employs over 700 people in its Remote Processing Center.
Largely concerned with traffic. As one employee put it, "Sure it's empty around here. But I'm home in ten minutes!" Support for the workout room, daycare center, and beer garden is near unanimous. Many support the hotbox, in the hopes that it will foster a "more lively office environment."

SUSIE HUANG, FISHKILL CLEANERS
Susie operates Fishkill Cleaners, one of three tenants in the Dutchess Mall. By default, the cleaners has become a bus stop.
Sees potential for a symbiotic relationship with the gym. Claims "One has to clean what one changes out of." Because oil-based paints wreak havoc on her washers, she is less enthusiastic about the studios.

SOUR CREEK SAND AND GRAVEL
Company (Sour Creek) has plan to mine the large hill immediately to the west of the mall.
"How many hiking trails do they need up here? This mountain is a gold mine, or at least a sand and gravel mine." Regarding other developments, cares little, but urges that the less that happens, the better. "More people means more complaints - it's an industry standard."

STEVE, STEVE'S HOTDOGS
Steve owns a hot dog cart that he operates from the front of the parking lot.
Generally in favor of anything that will bring more traffic to the parking lot, though he insists that gyms and hot dogs don't mix. Plus, artists are poor and they love hot dogs.

FLEA MARKET VENDORS
Vendors come from hundreds of miles to sell their goods at the Dutchess County Flea Market, on of the biggest in the state.
Vendors are wildly ecstatic about the summer stage, which they think will draw even bigger crowds to the flea market. One added "standing out there all day can get so boring. I'd love the chance to hear some live music."

SCENIC HUDSON
Local preservation group that is dedicated to preserving the "historic Hudson Valley."
"How many mines do they need up here? This mountain is too beautiful to mine!" Adds that it's one of the last remaining habitats of the timber rattlesnake. Agree with the miners though, that the less that happens the better. "Housing and small business belong downtown, not on the strip."

LOCALS
Think that southern Dutchess is already overpopulated, and don't want anything that might encourage immigration. And artist studios in Fishkill? There goes the neighborhood!

WEEKENDERS
Southern Dutchess has experienced an influx of New York City weekenders, who are increasingly buying up houses in towns like Beacon, where the Dia Center for the Arts will be opening a museum in Spring, 2002.
"A studio in an old shopping mall? And I thought warehouses were cool. But they're so over, don't you think?"

DMV
The Department if Motor Vehicles conducts A driving test in the parking lot.
Don't do a thing! That's the consensus from DMV bureaucrats. "The last thing these kids need is a carwash to navigate around," notes one. Have already made numerous complaints to the town about the mall's erratic, non-linear traffic patterns, which "tend to confuse the hell out of the drivers."

WAR MONUMENT: . . . I see a great civic square . . . boulevards radiating; and me, the center of it all!

DAYCARE CENTER: . . . From now on, developers will build daycare centers into everything. . .

Though condensed between the stages of design and completion, the conventional process of designing a building is time consuming, involving various stakeholders, planning processes and a wide team of consultants and contractors. What happens, though, if the time period of an architect's involvement is expanded? How might a more process-orientated approach shift the role of the architect? **Tobias Armborst, Daniel D'Oca and Georgeen Theodore**, principals of Interboro Partners in New York, describe how they have developed projects that have sought opportunities in expanding the timescale and remit of traditional practice.

Tobias Armborst,
Daniel D'Oca and
Georgeen Theodore

Architecture takes time. The process of establishing a programme, putting together the financing, getting stakeholders on board, and developing, representing and evaluating design alternatives is a long and often messy one. Inevitably this process has its ups and downs, dramatic turns and moments of revelation, and involves many different actors, forces and materials. As soon as the drama concludes with the completion of a building, a new act begins: tenants move in, repairs have to be made, new users have new ideas about form and function, and they transform the building accordingly.

However, while this drama of architecture-as-process unfolds over time, all of its entertaining twists, turns and transformations remain invisible to the readers of most architectural books and journals. There they see the building in its timeless beauty, photographed at the very moment of completion, before any human inhabitation leaves its traces. Philipp Oswalt has observed that in architectural thinking 'a distinctive division between production and consumption still dominates, finding expression not the least in the idea of the heroic highpoint that a building reaches when it is finished and becomes operational. … Everything that comes after completion is perceived as decline and degradation.'[1]

Cultivating an understanding of architecture-as-process is therefore highly relevant for architects. It can allow us to participate in decisions before and after the conventional time period of the architect's responsibilities, and thereby exert greater influence over the outcome. A number of Interboro Partners'

Interboro Partners,
In the Meantime,
Life With Landbanking,
Fishkill,
New York,
2003

The axonometric depicts the project's physical interventions (notated in yellow) during the landbanking phase, along with speculations about how on-site and off-site constituents might respond (shown in the 'quote' bubbles). Also included are future constituents (encircled by text). Finally, the interventions themselves dream about their future lives.

recent projects illustrate an expanded, process-oriented architecture along with new ways of representing such processes.

In the Meantime

While a limited duration is typically seen as an impediment to architecture, it can also be an opportunity. In the Meantime, Life with Landbanking, Interboro's winning submission for a 2002 ideas competition about dead shopping malls, was a reimagining of the shuttered Dutchess County Mall in Fishkill, New York, that proposed taking advantage of a particular moment in time ripe for formal and programmatic experimentation. The project began with a conversation with the mall's owner, who was landbanking the property. His plan was to sit on it and wait for property values to increase, at which point he would either redevelop or sell it. This decision to temporarily 'write off' the property was self-serving, and clearly not in the best interest of local residents who had to deal with the negative externalities associated with living near a large, decaying structure. But this landbanking phase – during which the owner was not paying any attention to the mall – had also opened opportunities for local residents to use the mall and its parking lot to do things they were unable to do elsewhere.

Indeed, spending time observing the mall's parking lot revealed a number of activities that were quite practical: for example, an ad-hoc flea market, dog walking, vending and cruising. Inspired by these activities, instead of a large-scale vision Interboro proposed spaces and programmes that would be impossible under the conditions of permanence: a collection of small, cheap, feasible interventions including a business incubator, fitness centre, daycare facility, sculpture park and summer stage. These would help nurture the cultures already starting to grow, and could lead to a future in which such programmes could thrive and prosper. To describe this process, Interboro developed a representational technique to illustrate the multiple times of the project. The axonometric not only visualises the conditions and actors already on the site during the landbanking period, but also projects possible programmes and stakeholders of the future.

The Power of Impermanence

In LentSpace (2009–11), one of a series of subsequent temporary public space projects, Interboro was able to build a tree nursery in New York's SoHo neighbourhood – something that would likely be inconceivable given the 'highest and best use' rubric that would have dominated the design of a more permanent project.

Temporary projects also require consideration of what happens to the architecture when its time is up. This often means finding community partners who can adopt the various elements of the project once it is disassembled. In some cases, in order to make the elements better suit the needs of such partners, Interboro has actively involved them in the design of the project itself. In addition to generating no waste, this process gives community members more of a stake in – and ultimately more ownership of – the project, which can in turn lead to increased use.

For example, for the *Commonplace* installation in the courtyard of the US Pavilion at the Venice Architecture Biennale 2012, Interboro designed and built a simple, accessible 'outdoor living room' for hanging out, as well as for Biennale-related programmes. Consisting of a platform that elevated the courtyard to the level of the interior gallery, and a few dozen foam stools that could be packed into the platform at the end of each day, Commonplace provided a casual, quiet backdrop to the colourful installations and programmes of the exhibition. To ensure that the platform would be reused when the Biennale was over, it was designed according to the specs of the temporary, elevated sidewalks – *passerelle* – that Venetians use to navigate the city during *acqua alta*, the regularly occuring high waters. When the project was disassembled, these *passerelle* were donated to the City of Venice in exchange for the metal stands the city had donated to hold them in place for the duration of the Biennale. The colourful, soft seating elements

left: LentSpace, commissioned by the Lower Manhattan Cultural Council, was constructed on a privately owned development site temporarily made open to the public. With a small construction budget, it was conceived as a temporary 'in the meantime' project to animate a vacant site awaiting renewal, offering a new model for land use citywide.

middle left: For the *Commonplace* installation, Interboro borrowed the standard-issue temporary, elevated sidewalks called *passerelle* that Venetians use to navigate the city during *acqua alta*, the regularly occurring high waters, and recombined them to transform the US Pavilion courtyard into an outdoor living room.

bottom: The project as represented both during and after the Biennale. Above: The *passerelle* (in light orange) and cubes (in dark orange) transformed the courtyard of the US Pavilion into an outdoor living room. Below: Venice's plaza playgrounds and sidewalks after the Biennale, when the project was disassembled and its components distributed throughout the city.

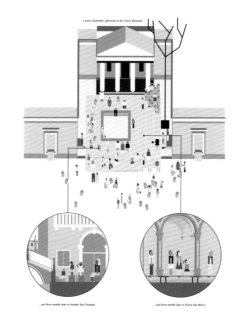

that were part of *Commonplace* were donated to city schools. The bartering and recycling involved in the implementation of the project were represented by appropriating elements from the graphic novel, a medium that offers many visual techniques for explaining a process in simple terms.

Hold It

In addition to representing architecture-as-process in drawings and diagrams, in *Holding Pattern* (2011), the winning competition entry to the MoMA PS1 Young Architects Program (YAP), Interboro made the process of developing, using and reusing architecture visible and tangible in space by designing an installation out of objects that were temporarily 'held' on their way to a new use. Every year, MoMA PS1 in Queens, New York, holds this competition to temporarily transform its courtyard into an environment for its celebrated 'Warm Up' summer music series. The brief is simple: provide seating, shade and a water feature for the roughly 6,000 visitors who visit Warm Up concerts every Saturday between June and September. The selected architect has to design, build and install everything in four months. Come autumn, when Warm Up is over, the project is disassembled.

MoMA PS1 is a generous institution that engages the surrounding community in numerous ways, but in others it feels detached from this vibrant, diverse neighbourhood. The 5-metre (16-foot) tall concrete wall the museum built along its property line on Jackson Avenue emphasises the divide between culture and neighbourhood, and is despised by the local community board. And in highlighting the most up-to-date music, the Warm Up summer concert series itself tends to attract a fairly homogeneous crowd of cool hipsters. Interboro's proposal therefore focused on ways in which the YAP might be used to undermine this institutional divide and strengthen connections between MoMA PS1 and its neighbours. The solution was to design and build something that could be put to a different use once the event was over.

The inspiration for the project was an existing makeshift plaza at the edge of a taxi stand that operates across the street from MoMA PS1. Consisting of a simple awning, a few plastic chairs and tables, and some plants, the manager of the Checker Cab taxi stand had built the plaza to give the drivers a place to hang out and relax between shifts. However, though popular, it required some improvement: the chairs were

Interboro Partners,
Holding Pattern,
MoMA PS1,
Long Island City,
Queens,
New York,
2011

right: The inspiration for *Holding Pattern* was a small, informal seating area on the Checker Cab taxi stand opposite MoMA PS1. The 5-metre (16-foot) walls of MoMA PS1 can be seen in the background.

below: Objects commissioned by some of MoMA PS1's Long Island City neighbours were 'held' in the museum's courtyard during the summer of 2011, forming an eclectic collection of things, including mirrors, ping-pong tables, a lifeguard chair, rock-climbing wall and many trees.

Interboro made the process of developing, using and reusing architecture visible and tangible in space by designing an installation out of objects that were temporarily 'held' on their way to a new use.

in need of repair, the plants were not exactly thriving, and the awning was full of holes.

It became apparent that the Warm Up's needs – seating and shade – were not necessarily different from those of its neighbours. So, instead of designing and building an object that would end up in the dumpster, Interboro proposed designing an installation out of objects that people in the neighbourhood could use. The objects could be 'held' in the MoMA PS1 courtyard during the summer, where they would be enjoyed by Warm Up patrons, then be given to their 'new' owners in the autumn.

Over the following weeks, after discussions and meetings with representatives of dozens of institutions including schools, senior citizens centres, public housing projects, local businesses, libraries and post offices, Interboro was able to compile a list of needed items and select those that would work well in the MoMA PS1 courtyard during the Warm Up. The *Holding Pattern* elements were then designed so that they would meet the local institutions' needs, but also create unique spatial experiences. They were installed in the courtyard of MoMA PS1 during the summer, but what is usually the end of the Young Architects Program was for *Holding Pattern* only the beginning. Once disassembled in the autumn, more than 50 organisations in Long Island City received 79 objects and 84 trees.

This process allowed Interboro to expand the audience, budget, programme and shelf life of the project, and present a reusable model for the design of temporary environments. Traditionally, the YAP has one client (MoMA PS1), one designer (the architects), a limited audience (patrons of the Warm Up summer concert series), a small budget, a simple programme (seating, shade and a water feature) and a limited shelf life (three months). *Holding Pattern* changed this formula, and in so doing created a new model for the design of temporary environments. Here, the YAP went from one client to more than 50.

The project also had multiple authors: asking local institutions to nominate the ingredients gave them a sense of ownership. In part as a result of this, the YAP audience became much broader: because they were involved in the creation of the project, the local institutions Interboro worked with were more interested in it, and were more likely to attend the museum (which, it turned out, many in

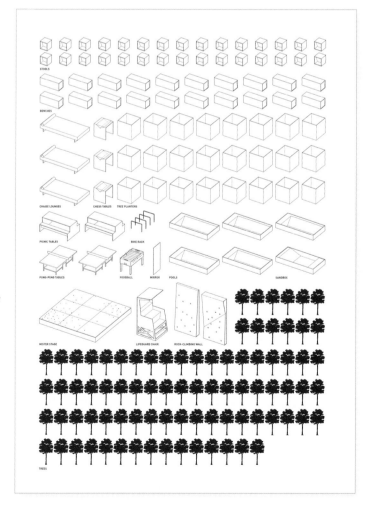

Interboro Partners,
Holding Pattern,
MoMA PS1,
Long Island City,
Queens,
New York,
2011

opposite top and middle: In the spring, the Long Island City School of Ballet requested eight mirrors. In the summer they were installed in the Mirror Room in a side yard of MOMA PS1. In the autumn the mirrors were installed in the ballet school's new dance studio.

opposite bottom: An inventory of all of the items held at *Holding Pattern* during the summer of 2011, including 79 pieces of furniture and 84 trees. A unified formal language gave coherence to the assemblage of diverse objects, and continues to keep the objects recognisable as components of *Holding Pattern* throughout Queens.

above right: A free newspaper featured short portraits introducing Interboro's partner organisations in Long Island City, along with a map showing the distribution of all the objects and trees that were held at *Holding Pattern* during the summer of 2011.

below: To visualise and explain the concept of *Holding Pattern*, Interboro commissioned the illustrator Lesser Gonzalez Alvarez to develop a large mural for the museum's courtyard. Using the graphic language of cartoons, the mural shows the different stages of the project in one synchronised illustration.

the neighbourhood had previously found intimidating). This enriched the diversity of the space. Finally, while the project was only supposed to last for a few months, *Holding Pattern* became a project without a foreseeable end. The local institutions are still making use of the trees, benches, ping-pong tables and other objects they received, and the Long Island City wider public is still benefiting from this neighbourhood improvement project in disguise.

To explain the temporal nature of *Holding Pattern* to museum visitors, Interboro employed a number of representational techniques such as 'hold'-tags, museum labels, a large mural, and a free newspaper with articles introducing the different neighbourhood organisations that had commissioned elements of the installation.

Harnessing the power of process requires being less concerned with the 'timeless' perfection of completed products and much more with the acts of defining, developing, transforming and even recycling projects. Though working this way is messy, and is characterised by a lot of muddling through and making do, the approach has proved to be as much an opportunity as a limitation. ⌀

Note
1. Philipp Oswalt, 'Pre- and Post-Architecture', *Harvard Design Magazine*, 37, 2014, p 41.

Jonathan Mallie

Ever Faster

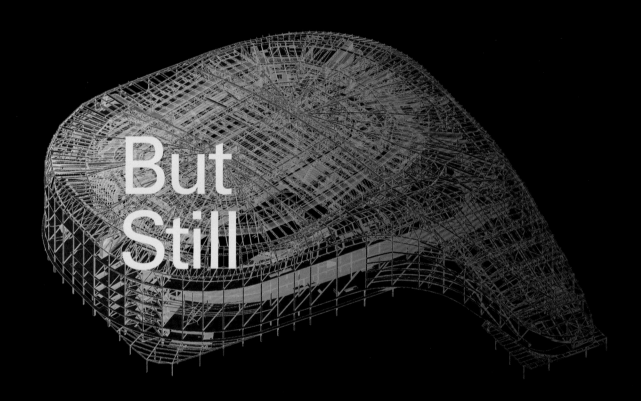

But Still

Very Good

360 Architecture and
Thornton Tomasetti,
Roger's Place,
Edmonton,
Alberta,
due for completion 2016–17

Completing a building on time at a high quality is an age-old challenge for design and construction professionals. But what happens when everything speeds up exponentially? **Jonathan Mallie** is an expert in integrating design innovation with technologically advanced construction solutions. The founder of JLM | design & construction consultancy, he was previously a principal at SHoP in New York. Here he describes how 4D and 5D building information modelling (BIM) technologies allow architects to build quickly in response to clients' needs for speed, but also benefit the design- and-build process.

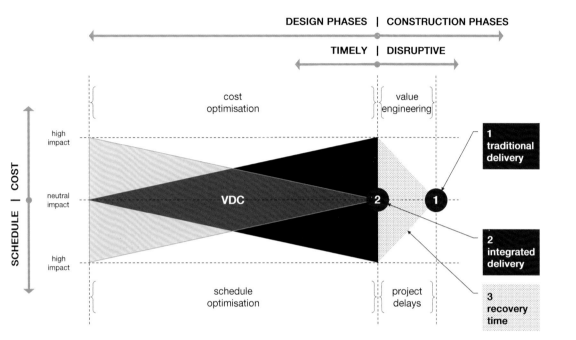

JLM | design & construction consultancy, Project delivery diagram, 2015

The integrated delivery process of virtual design and construction (VDC) allows for timely cost and schedule optimisation during the design phases, avoiding the disruptive value engineering and project delays that typically occur after completion of the design in traditional project delivery.

The realities of today's economics, coupled with the possibilities now inherent in the latest design and construction technologies, have created a 'speed to construction' movement in architecture. This is not to say that the goal of building owners is to reduce the time the design takes, but rather that the start of construction has become a widely sought-after project milestone. As many owners look to reduce the overall duration of building projects, it has become increasingly prevalent for design time to be overlapped or integrated with construction time. When properly orchestrated, the integration of these phases can enhance both the design and the project as a whole, which becomes greater than the sum of its parts: a 1 + 1 = 3 model.

Owners are pressured by various financial factors that in turn influence their timelines for project delivery. On the one hand, longer-term owners of projects that yield returns over the course of decades, such as multi-family residential buildings, place less emphasis on the start of construction and instead focus on the duration of the construction phase as it relates to the time when the residential units become available in the marketplace. On the other hand, there exists a subset of owners who are responsible for commissioning the design, construction and operation of buildings and must meet shorter-term scheduling demands such as starting construction on particular dates at specific times of year.

Among other building typologies, sports and entertainment venues stand out as prime examples of projects that must be completed within a precisely scheduled period of time and by a particular date. In the world of sports architecture, team and building owners make commitments to their home cities and fan bases that their teams will, for example, 'play on opening day'. This means that there is simply no room for delays nor opportunities to 'push the schedule out' by a season or two, either when building a new sports venue or renovating an existing one. Fixed event dates thus become key in the establishment of constraint-based design criteria.

Traditionally, constraints such as cost thresholds or schedule milestones have been considered to be inhibitors to the design process. Is it possible, instead, that these factors may contribute to more informed, and in many cases better design? Arguably, success in architecture is not measured by the quality of an idea, but rather by its manifestation in the built environment. Buildings cost money. They take time to build. Therefore, in addition to measuring a project's success by the quality of the material used, its spatial characteristics and the ability to create meaningful human interaction, more pragmatic factors related to cost and schedule should also be considered, and with equal importance. The answers to the age-old questions 'Was it built on time?' and 'Was it built on budget?' should be a resounding yes.

Virtual Design and Construction

The adoption of current design and construction technologies provides a platform to maximise the ethereal qualities of materials and space through the management of the indelicate factors of cost and schedule. These technologies contribute to our digital 'tool chests', which have expanded beyond the virtual management of geometry (3D modelling) to include the virtual management of time (4D modelling) as well as quantity and cost information (5D modelling).

The feedback loop inherent in multidimensional digital modelling enables architects and engineers to meet the demands of today's most challenging projects. Through the implementation of various digital exercises, widely known as virtual design and construction (VDC), the construction phase can start on time without sacrificing quality, since the building is constructed virtually before actual realisation takes place. The input of invaluable information into the model from the design and construction teams reduces the time required for interpretation by their construction-side counterparts. Historically, such interpretive activities

ROSSETTI, Daytona Rising, Daytona International Speedway, Daytona, Florida, due for completion 2016

below left: The scope of the project included integration of the existing grandstand with sections of new grandstand, resulting in a stadium that spans nearly one linear mile and seats 101,000 fans.

below right: Building information models of the stadium section allowed the architects and the engineering team to review and coordinate building systems and structure in the virtual realm prior to completion of the design and the onset of construction.

have occurred during the tender or bid phase of traditional design-bid-build project delivery.

The architecture firm ROSSETTI and engineers Thornton Tomasetti represent design professionals who have achieved success by embracing technology to meet the project demands of their sports sector clients, combined with a willingness to compress the overall design and construction time period through the integration of the activities, phases and project teams of both. Daytona Rising is a US$400 million project to redevelop the Daytona International Speedway grandstand into an almost mile-long stadium with 101,500 seats, five injectors, 11 football-sized 'neighbourhoods' and three concourse levels, the complexity of which led ROSSETTI to implement advanced VDC techniques to manage the design and facilitate the construction.

ROSSETTI's approach to the VDC platform for Daytona Rising was to integrate and consolidate information, utilising it early on in the design process with a significant focus on constructability. VDC allowed for cutting through tedious data management and redundancies, and for

The approach to the VDC platform for Daytona Rising was to integrate and consolidate information, utilising it early on in the design process with a significant focus on constructability.

model-based design reviews by the owner that aided the decision-making process. With Autodesk's Revit® and Navisworks® serving as the dominant building information modelling (BIM) programs for the project, 3D modelling and coordination enabled design team collaborators to review progress virtually and to coordinate various building systems, such as electrical, plumbing, heating and cooling, and the building structure. ROSSETTI's 5D modelling initiative also drew from the design model a database of information about materials and quantities, and allowed for accurate quantity surveying to verify items such as cubic yardage of concrete, tonnage of structural steel, square footage of glazing and roofing materials, quantities of doors and metal panels, and railing and seating counts, all well before construction began.

Model Accuracy in Major Renovations

At the beginning of the construction documentation phase, the client, International Speedway Corporation (ISC), changed direction and decided to keep the existing grandstand's steel structure for the lower bowl and seating areas. To meet this request, a point cloud 3D laser scan was

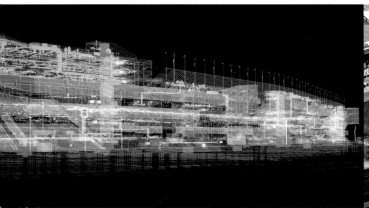

performed and used to create a model of the grandstand, which was incorporated into the new structural steel design for the enlarged seating area. The high-definition laser scan uncovered inconsistencies in the existing structure, providing a highly accurate model of actual conditions, which saved field measuring time that would otherwise have been required to document each anomalous condition. The process involved setting up a laser scan every 9 metres (30 feet) along the mile-long grandstand. This information was then converted into a 3D model that could be used by the project's structural engineers, Walter P Moore. According to ROSSETTI Technical Director Greg Sweeney, the data still required reconciliation with limited field surveys to obtain the most accurate information. However, the decision to keep the grandstand intact saved approximately 3,000 tons of steel and approximately $10 million while streamlining the construction sequence, as it allowed the original seating to remain untouched throughout the building process, becoming a permanent component of the newly renovated stadium.

During the construction phase, builders Barton Malow used models generated by ROSSETTI as a starting point for

their modelling programme, and subsequently required all major subcontractors to develop fabrication models as part of the project's VDC platform. Hyperlinked PDFs were utilised to distribute drawings, details, requests for information and submittals. iPads were used in the field to view the model and 2D documentation, and for adding notes to each in real time. Barton Malow's field office included multiple touchscreens and large video displays to provide digital connection to project documentation, which allowed all parties to efficiently coordinate the work and the client to understand the building virtually prior to construction. ROSSETTI's advanced VDC platform thus reduced the time necessary for problem solving in order to achieve timely project completion.

Advanced Structural Steel Detailing

The building structure, which is in many cases structural steel for sports development projects, is one of the key aspects of design that requires early resolution by the structural engineers prior to the completion of the design phases. For engineers Thornton Tomasetti, a main challenge is coordinating the commitments needed to advance early procurement and detailing packages. This requires the owner's commitment to make timely and informed decisions, and the design team's undertaking to streamline the flow of information to advance drawing packages with confidence that the design will not undergo significant change. Decision matrices and required information from each consultant require careful coordination among design team members to establish workflow efficiency.

Parametric modelling is often used to enable rapid iterations during concept design and through the subsequent design development phases. Fabrication modelling is also incorporated for early detailing, thus reducing the duration of the shop drawing phase and in some cases eliminating it altogether.

As seen in Thornton Tomasetti's US Bank Stadium in Minneapolis, which is scheduled for completion in 2016, software such as Trimble's Tekla® continues to blur the distinction between design and fabrication. For this home for National Football League (NFL) team the Minnesota Vikings, Thornton Tomasetti used Tekla to compile structural steel mill order information and to create a connected model, providing a complete level of structural steel detailing prior to delivery to the fabricator. By moving the detailed structural steel modelling forward in time, the engineers shifted what is otherwise a downstream activity to the design phase of the project. In the case of the Vikings' stadium, the result was a major reduction in activity during the construction phase, coupled with a reduction of the contractor's responsibility to interpret and translate the design, therefore potentially improving the quality of the work.

Thornton Tomasetti has also implemented parametric modelling tools that allow the architectural and structural design teams to work in parallel at early stages of a project and to determine critical design parameters such as building form and geometry. For 360 Architecture's Roger's Place project, the new home of the Edmonton Oiler in Edmonton, Alberta and due to be completed before the 2016–17

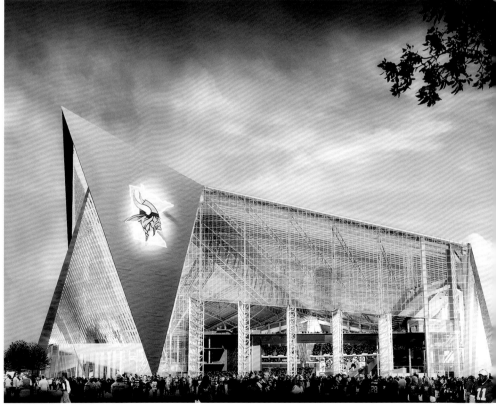

National Hockey League (NHL) season, the engineers used parametric modelling tools such as Grasshopper® (a plug-in for the prevalent 3D modelling software Rhinoceros) that allowed optimal structural parameters to be married with optimal architectural criteria that were worked through in tandem.

Through rapid iteration and testing, advanced parametric tools provide opportunities for design resolution early on, enabling the project to advance as an integrated whole. Maximising the benefits of parametric modelling requires that the project team is fully committed to the architectural programme, is able to work precisely with 3D geometry, and makes a timely selection of materials. Ideally, decisions build upon one another linearly to support overall design production. Recovering from nonlinear decision paths greatly challenges project success.

Quality must not be threatened or sacrificed to achieve sufficient speed to construction. However, the utilisation of advanced software not only decreases the time needed to begin construction, it also allows for the consistent infusion of construction-related information into the design process, which in many cases can increase the possibility for art and beauty to emerge. VDC enables a higher level of detailing and refinement, and also minimises the challenges inherent in more traditional contracting methods where risk is shifted to a 'receiving party' who is challenged to interpret the designer's intentions.

Still Analogue, Too

The exponential increase in the use of advanced software, coupled with technologically driven design and construction solutions, and the growing requirement for speed to construction, also reveal an ever-pressing need to retain somewhat analogue methods of communication. Video conferencing and online meetings using platforms such as Skype, GoTo Meeting and Webex have greatly enhanced communication. However, the facilitation of communication through such devices is simply not the same as being in the same room, making 'true' eye contact and, in many cases, reading body language as ways to interpret the position, intentions and interests of one's collaborators. Since the building industry still operates in an adversarial and litigious realm, due to its contracting methods and legal structure, highly effective ways to communicate need to be implemented that will allow the building of strong interpersonal relationships and trust. People remain the key ingredient. Put the right team in the room with the right VDC toolset and an appropriate level of design and construction integration, and you have a winner – the manifestation of renaissance master building merged with 21st-century technology that will also put the spirit back into design and construction. ⌀

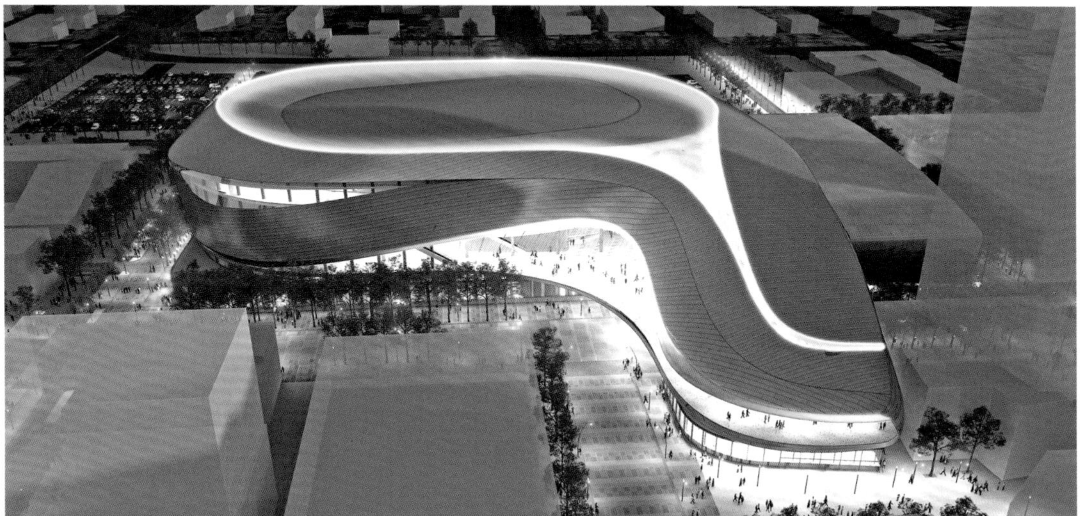

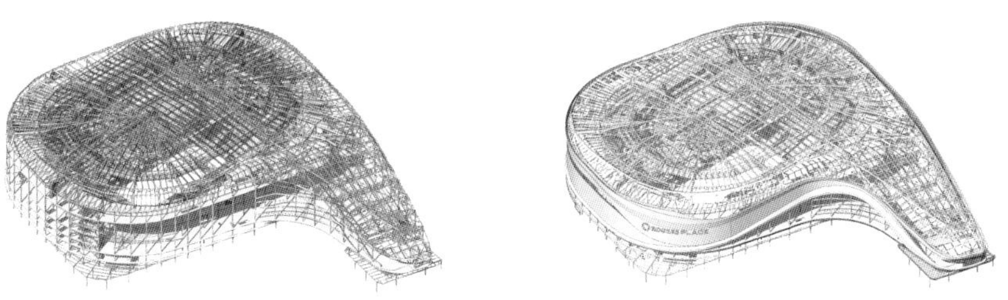

360 Architecture and Thornton Tomasetti, Roger's Place, Edmonton, Alberta, due for completion 2016-17

top: Working closely with 360 Architecture, Thornton Tomasetti developed structural engineering criteria for the proposed multipurpose arena that will serve as the new home for the National Hockey League's Edmonton Oilers.

bottom: The architectural and structural models for the arena were consolidated in Autodesk's Revit® for the purposes of advanced 3D coordination.

No More Stopping

ARNHEM CENTRAAL

UNStudio,
Arnhem Central Masterplan,
Arnhem,
The Netherlands,
2015

One way architects can remain engaged with their projects over time is by completing buildings originally conceived as part of a larger-scale masterplan, as UNStudio has done over the last 20 years for the Arnhem Central station. As part of a planning commission originally received in 1996, the firm has realised a bus terminal and underground car park, as well as a series of platform roofs for rail passengers.

The dissolution of the conventional breaking points in the construction and completion phases of a building's delivery has blurred 'the distinction between the production of design intent and the transmission of information'. Here **Richard Garber**, Director of the School of Architecture at the New Jersey Institute of Technology (NJIT), advocates that architects should use this as an opportunity to widen their remit, gaining agency and with it responsibility and the financial rewards to practice. Here he draws from the examples of UNStudio, GLUCK+ and his own New-York based practice, GRO Architects.

In the past architects have faced at least two stopping points: between design and construction, and at a building's completion. Recent advances in computer software in architecture have removed these stopping points, and so significantly expanded the role of architects and, as importantly, extended the period of time they can remain engaged with the projects they design. Stopping has long been an issue in architecture, inherent to practice. Where the stops are placed on a project both defines and limits an architect's time and operational territory. This has a qualitative as well as a quantitative impact. Allocation of time is synonymous with design quality, agency, responsibility and economic remuneration. For centuries, the stopping point was at the completion of a drawing set: how much information should the drawings contain was often a subject of negotiation between architect and client. Now, with the onset of the digital, there is no longer a distinction between the production of design intent and the transmission of information.[1]

From 1994 to 2004, animation software offered architects the chance to generate an endless array of tantalising formal possibilities, raising the challenge of when to stop and why. And, during that period it was difficult, if not impossible, for architects to move from forms achieved through animation to construction because both clients and builders were doubtful about the form's constructability, since the software being used for animation was not intended to guide physical construction. As a consequence, architects with digital ambitions used design competitions such as the Yokohama Port Terminal and Cardiff Bay Opera House to produce projects that were seen as remarkable but unbuildable. While notable projects were ultimately built, including the Presbyterian Church of New York by Greg Lynn FORM with Douglas Garofalo and Michael McInturf (1999), most remained exclusively exciting digital speculations, stopping at design and publication.

Then, auspiciously, the 4D and 5D tools of building information modelling (BIM), broadly adopted around 2004, allowed for continuity from conceptual design explorations through construction. Architects can now convey their design intentions virtually to builders, as well as a technological knowledge transfer to local contractors. Since about 2010, virtual models have extended architects' involvement even further by offering them opportunities to manage, evaluate and maintain a building throughout its lifetime. For example, UNStudio was part of a consortium that will remain engaged in the management and maintenance of the Education Executive Agency and Tax Offices building they designed in Groningen, the Netherlands, for a period of 20 years, at which point the building can be transformed into housing, a possible future that had to be conceived early in the design of the project.

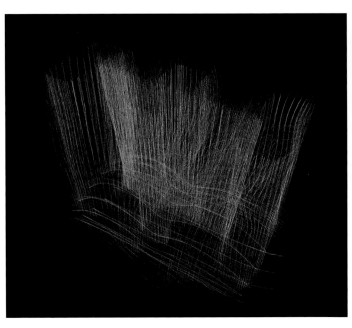

Richard Garber,
Tower scheme,
Brooklyn,
New York,
2002

In the late 1990s, when architects used animation software for manipulations of geometry that allowed a form to change over time, it was difficult to judge why one form might be better than another. Those critical of such formal exercises called this the 'stopping problem'. In the scheme illustrated here, conceived while Richard Garber was employed at SHoP Architects, the towers were also colour scaled using an RGB formula coordinated with the amount of deformation.

UNStudio,
Education Executive Agency
and Tax Offices,
Groningen,
The Netherlands,
2011

UNStudio worked with a design-build-operate team not only to deliver the building, but also to maintain its operation for a period of 20 years following its completion in 2011. The decision to convert the project housing after two decades forced the architects to make long-term decisions about the design that would not usually be included in typical architectural services.

UNStudio,
Arnhem Central Transfer Hall,
Arnhem,
The Netherlands,
2015

Arnhem Transfer Hall is the central building in the Arnhem Central Masterplan that UNStudio has worked on since 1996. The architects created a data-transfer workflow to provide the glass-fibre reinforced concrete precast panel fabricator, mxB, with all the information they needed to invent a reconfigurable mould that was used to produce some 1,500 unique cladding panels.

This view of the roof shows the tolerances the precast fabricator was able to achieve using the reconfigurable mould.

UNStudio generated a series of VisualBasic scripts within Rhinoceros 3D modelling software to extract dimensional data from the series of 21 points for each panel. The data was transmitted electronically to the installer, Sorba Projects, who added further information for the substructure. The dataset was then sent as a comma-separated values (.CSV) file to the precast fabricator who used laser projection and a series of magnets to reconfigure the casting mould to produce each specific panel contour and perimeter shape.

Non-Stop Workflows

The advent of BIM effectively removed the barriers architects had previously faced when there was a hard stop between tendering contract documents by the architect and construction of the building by the general contractor. In this model, the architect had limited exposure to on-site construction processes or to those people involved in the fabrication of components and materials. In addition to the possibility of enhanced collaboration between the design and construction teams, architects utilising BIM tools can now realise continuity through the organising of virtual data (including geometry) – performance simulation – through the fabrication of building components, project scheduling and transmission of data for construction.

As BIM is a graphic database of the architect's design intent and the geometry and building components it informs, architects working in the 21st century have become increasingly sophisticated in the way they manage data and its flows to others on the design and construction team. From its beginnings as a concept in the manufacturing schemas of the industrialising world, such workflows not only define a related scope of work between parties over time, but also increasingly include specific ways in which these parties interact.

UNStudio has built itself around several core research platforms that redefine how an architect's design intentions fit into an overall project workflow, as exemplified in the Arnhem Central Transfer Hall (2015). The hall is the principal piece of the Arnhem Central Masterplan, which UNStudio completed in the late 1990s. Realising individual buildings, originally conceived as parts of a planning project, over the course of 20 years is certainly one way architects can remain engaged with their projects over time.

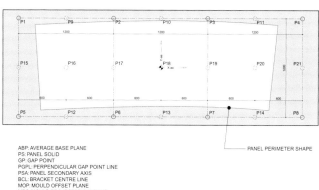

ABP: AVERAGE BASE PLANE
PS: PANEL SOLID
GP: GAP POINT
PGPL: PERPENDICULAR GAP POINT LINE
PSA: PANEL SECONDARY AXIS
BCL: BRACKET CENTRE LINE
MOP: MOULD OFFSET PLANE
MPC: MOULD PROJECTED CONTOUR
MRCS: MOULD RIB CUT SURFACE
PLA: PANEL LONGITUDINAL AXIS
POP: PANEL ORIGIN POINT

PANEL PERIMETER SHAPE

Working closely with UNStudio, the panel fabricator, mxB, devised a reconfigurable mould that was constrained by 21 individual points that were adjusted by measurements taken from the architects' Rhinoceros model. Among the various dimensions required by the fabricator were axis points, contour offsets and perimeter shape conditions that UNStudio provided in a spreadsheet.

For the design of the hall, UNStudio worked very closely with the fabricators and installers, utilising their design model directly in the fabrication process of the roof panels. In this case the designers found a creative way to engage the precast subcontractor directly through the transfer of information from their model. Here, the design model was not simply used for the tendering of documentation, but was extended directly into the fabrication process through data extraction, which in turn produced a flexible mould system for the building's glass-fibre reinforced concrete roof panels. This case demonstrates how the variations explored in the 1990s through animation can now be quantified and specified for fabricators. Geometry was always precise and measurable in the computer. Now, through data translation, it is buildable.

The Arnhem Central Transfer Hall links distinct transit modes together in the railway station complex, including pedestrians, trains and local and regional buses. A large car parking garage exists below it, and two office towers sit above, giving the west side of the building a fairly rigid gridded layout that is intertwined with the east side where all the various transit modes come together. During the planning phase, the building was imagined as a concrete shell with some steel trusses. However, following the document tendering, the contractor, Bouwcombinatie Ballast Nedam, proposed a steel roof structure with a glass-fibre reinforced concrete cladding. In working with the contractors, UNStudio rationalised the structure and were also able to determine how to make the panelling more feasible and cost-effective.

In rationalising the panelling system, a workflow was invented that would seamlessly transmit precise digital sizes and dimensions from the design model to the fabrication beds of the fabricator. UNStudio worked with mbX, an innovative precast company, to create a series of scripts that would extract the necessary data from their Rhinoceros model and format them in a spreadsheet for the fabrication team to use. This workflow allowed for 98 per cent of the approximately 1,500 panels to be formed in a flexible mould that contained a total of 21 point locations, and was hydraulically adjusted and held in place with magnets to achieve the various panel shapes. The extraction of information and the invention of the flexible mould were novel, yet the instructions to build were quite simple. These operations pre-empted a stop in the flow of information between the designer and the subcontractor. Sorba Projects, a facade engineer and installer, engaged mbX in the fabrication process and installed the panels on the building's steel frame.

In this project, as in many projects where BIM is employed, there was no stopping between design and fabrication, in that the information model, first as a design model and then as a fabrication model, provided all the data necessary to go directly into fabrication and no tendering of shop drawings or other production was required. The design team wrote tools in VisualBasic for Rhinoceros 3D to extract specific data and measurements from the model for the flexible steel mould system. No geometry was transmitted to the fabricators, and in effect the data went directly from model to mould.

Building+

BIM allows for enhanced collaboration between the architect-led design team and the construction subcontractors while the building is being constructed. Data conceived using BIM during the design phases can subsequently provide information for monitoring a building's performance after it is completed. The question then arises: Who makes decisions based on a reading of that operation data? The architect is certainly one candidate for that role.

And indeed, architects, or at least the virtual models they develop in the service of the design-to-construction process, have found an afterlife in the world of life-cycle assessment and management (LCA+M). Increasingly, these models are being used to manage buildings over time, often in their daily operation. Such monitoring can occur for relatively short periods, such as a year or two to ensure proper commissioning of the mechanical system, or over longer periods that may coincide with a 20-year or 30-year financial agreement.

Large teams of designers, builders and operators are now participating in the execution of design-build-operate (DBO) contracts, which are becoming increasingly popular in the US and Europe for institutions such as universities and government agencies. Under such agreements, a private-sector team provides design, construction and operation services under a turnkey contract that includes provisions for the operation of the building over a period of time. These agreements emerged in the early 1990s as public-private partnerships (PPP's) for large-scale infrastructure projects such as roadways or ports. However, the ability to simulate physical capacities of buildings, such as their energy consumption or lighting

GLUCK+,
The East Harlem School,
New York,
2008

During the post-occupancy calibration of the building's mechanical system, the school board decided that, to reduce costs, the system should be simplified so as not to heat or cool the building in the spring and autumn. About two years after the building was occupied, the system was retrofitted to allow for fresh air without the requisite cooling and heating, and the cost savings have been significant.

output, within a BIM makes it useful at the operational level of smaller-scale buildings as well. In effect, BIM transitions from a design tool to a construction tool to an operational one.

Peter Gluck uses an analogue version of BIM, which he calls Architect-Led Design-Build (ALDB). He has been outspoken about the traditional divisions between architecture and construction and how post-occupancy is understood. His firm GLUCK+ regularly enters into contracts to both design and build their projects, and is increasingly involved in the operational activities of their completed buildings in the years following client occupation, becoming an example of a DBO architectural practice. Since the design team leads the entire process, from concept to construction completion, team members can analyse, interpret and respond to post-occupancy issues with immediacy.

ALDB has allowed Gluck to stay involved with projects beyond the traditional point of drawing tender. He does this for the success of the project, achieving better design at lower cost through the coordination of individual building trades and construction sequencing. In the case of the East Harlem School, this process allowed the project team to forgo use of funds allocated for construction contingency while bringing the final cost of construction in at US$500,000 under the guaranteed maximum price, which was then applied to the school's endowment. Given the success of the project, Gluck was invited to join the school's Board of Trustees, and he continues to be involved in its post-occupancy operation. He pursues this role with institutional projects as well as individual houses, and maintains professional relationships with clients in both cases.

Better design at lower cost through the coordination of individual building trades and construction sequencing

In 2005, GLUCK+ designed and built the Bar House in the Colorado Rockies, and then a guest residence, the House in the Mountains, on the same site in 2014. The guesthouse incorporates an intricate solar hot water system that heats the pool during the day and the house at night. Through metrics and remote monitoring, the design team realised that the solar hot water system was not working as efficiently as it could post-occupancy, leading them to set new benchmarks on the system's thermometer. Charlie Kaplan, the project architect for GLUCK+, conceived a thickened wall of millwork that the solar hot water panels would clad on the south-facing 'service side' of the project, providing an accessible cavity for the plumbing system.[2] The system is a 'drainback system': rather than taking hot water into a service tank, it is injected directly into a hot water loop that feeds the swimming pool, living space and hot tub. The team wanted to circumvent the use of the boiler so decided to programme an override into the system. On sunny days, the solar hot water system would continue operating to heat water up to 30°C (86°F), so at night the water temperature of the pool would not fall below 28°C (82°F) and force the boiler on. In effect, the team found that overheating the pool, while still keeping it within the comfort zone of swimming, would deliver energy savings in that the boilers would not be used during the summer months.

During 'normal' design or construction stages, it would have been impossible to understand such intricacies in the way the solar hot water system and boiler would work together. The solution came post-occupancy through the architect's understanding of how the clients were using the system and when they were using the pool. Gluck refers to this post-construction responsibility for a project as 'staying with these buildings', and gives each owner an operational manual of sorts that is produced six to eight months after the building is occupied. According to him, this is 'defensive on one hand as most mechanical systems don't work quite properly when first commissioned'.[3] The conventional solution is to bring in a third party, typically a mechanical subcontractor not previously involved with the project, to 'fix it', which further complicates what is generally a problem of 'dialing the system' to get it to perform as designed.

This example also reveals the degree of coordination many architects are beginning to require in the execution of work. GLUCK+, as architect, facilitated collaboration between all parties who worked on the pool system: a plumbing subcontractor, a controls subcontractor, a control system manufacturer and a mechanical engineer. The high level at which the mechanical system now performs would have been 'impossible to achieve on the front end' according to Kaplan.[4]

GLUCK+,
House in the Mountains,
Colorado Rockies,
2012

The swimming pool created a large heating load, and it became clear once the house was occupied that seasonal strategies would need to be implemented to optimise the solar hot water system. Colorado has a very specific and varied climate. In the summer the heat load on the living spaces is minimal, so there is no benefit to the system in terms of heating them in the summer months.

The south-facing 'service side' of the house has automobile access to the garage as well as a cavity wall outfit with solar hot water panels that heat both the living spaces of the house and the pool.

Prior to the late 1990s, architects could expect only limited involvement during the construction of their designs, creating a disconnect of the architect from the construction site and marginalising the architect's role within the design and construction process. With the initial invention of computer-enabled design, architects were able to propose projects that piqued the interest of potential clients, but were not easily buildable. BIM has not only made construction of such works possible, but has allowed architects to play what is now a far more central and necessary role in managing both design and construction data between numerous parties. So there is no stopping between what had previously been discrete stages of designing and building. With the more recent advent of DBO schemes, architects can now engage owners and facility operators in post-construction actions to ensure that buildings perform, and continue to perform, as designed.

It is crucial that architects understand the opportunities such actions present. They extend our agency while allowing us to expand the territory of our work. No longer does design stop when the 'drawings are done' or even when the building is completed. We are entering a period of non-stop architecture. ⌂

Notes
1: Richard Garber, *BIM Design: Realising the Creative Potential of Building Information Modeling* (John Wiley & Sons (Chichester), 2014.
2: Conversation between the author and Peter Gluck, Charlie Kaplan and Stacie Wong, New York, 20 May 2015.
3: *Ibid.*
4: *Ibid.*

right: The wall cavity on the southern site provides a canted surface for the mounting of the solar hot water system that heats the interior spaces, spa and pool. The resultant triangular cavity contains all the piping to supply hot water to all areas in the house. The interior abutting the cavity is fitted with a wall of millwork, which provides storage. Finally a continuous clerestory window, fitted with a light.

below: The solar hot water system is used primarily to heat the swimming pool to a comfortable temperature during the summer. The nighttime air temperature can drop to 7˚C (45˚F), causing the pool to dip below its set point. The mechanical system's boiler automatically turns on to compensate. With a fine-tuning of the controls of the solar hot water system, the heat is stored from the last hours of sunlight in the late afternoon to heat the pool by a few degrees the next morning.

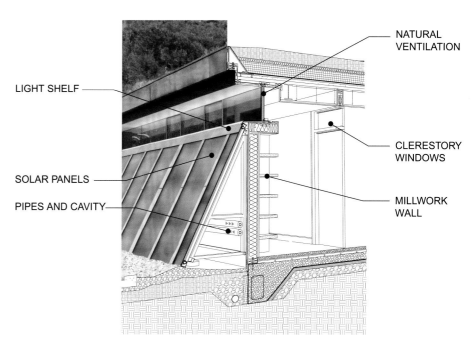

NATURAL VENTILATION

LIGHT SHELF

CLERESTORY WINDOWS

SOLAR PANELS

MILLWORK WALL

PIPES AND CAVITY

WALL ASSEMBLY

SOLAR HOT WATER SYSTEM
(SUMMER USAGE)

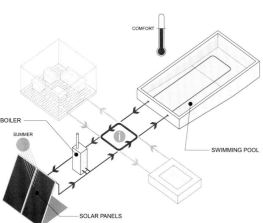

COMFORT

BOILER

SUMMER

SWIMMING POOL

SOLAR PANELS

Visiting Karsten Harries and Revisiting his 'Building and the Terror of Time'

Karsten Harries, Howard H Newman Professor of Philosophy at Yale University, has written one of the most influential essays reflecting on the relationship between time and architecture, 'Building and the Terror of Time' (1982). For Harries, architecture is a means of resisting mortality and coping with the fear of human transience. In order to reassess those ideas in the current context of this issue, Guest-Editor **Karen A Franck** interviewed Harries in the spring of 2015.

Pieter Bruegel the Elder,
The Tower of Babel,
1563

For Karsten Harries, Bruegel's painting illustrates the prideful desire to resist time by constructing monumental buildings that dominate time and space, but also another human desire: to create modest, human-scaled structures that are responsive to their neighbours, as shown nestled against the tower and making up the city below.

The philosopher Karsten Harries gave his essay of 1982 a powerful if not provocative title: 'Building and the Terror of Time'.[1] Given the relevance of that essay for this issue of ⌂, I took the opportunity to interview Professor Harries in his office at Yale University in May 2015, and then continued our conversation via email. These exchanges are drawn upon here, alongside a rereading of his essay and parts of his subsequent book, *The Ethical Function of Architecture* (1998).[2] For a more complete understanding of Karsten Harries's ideas and the many sources he draws from in philosophy, the Bible and art criticism, it is best to read his works themselves.

WHAT IS THE PROBLEM?
WHAT ARE SOME ALTERNATIVES?

For Harries, the 'terror of time' is, essentially, a universal, eminently human fear of mortality – of the eventual ending of life and, indeed, of all that has been made. He sees architecture as one of the ways that humanity addresses that fear. During our correspondence he wrote:

> I do think that the terror of time has its foundation in the human condition. As old as humanity is the concern with death and the need to cope with it. And from the very beginning architecture has figured centrally in coping strategies, which, to be sure, have taken very different forms at different times and in different places.

One fundamental response is to create shelter: 'Shelter promises protection from time's terror. To feel sheltered is to have banished feelings of vulnerability and mortality.'[3]

Shelter, however, is not sufficient. Stability and certainty are also sought; one means is through large-scale construction born of pride: 'as man finds it more and more difficult to interpret Nature as his home and takes it upon himself to defeat the terror of time with his own constructions … The dream of the engineer or the artist as god … is a dream born of pride.' Harries selects the Tower of Babel as depicted by Pieter Bruegel the Elder as the archetype of such constructions: the tower seeks to 'dominate space and time'. However, another architecture is also apparent: 'the much less ambitious architecture of the surrounding city' and 'modest shelters' nestled against the tower.[4]

In the essay's closing paragraph, Harries touches briefly on what the alternatives to building in the terror of time might be by referring again to Bruegel's painting:

> Here we have, not monuments, but buildings that speak of a very different, less antagonistic relationship to time. They hint at possibilities of dwelling born of a trust deeper than pride. Such trust demands determinations of beauty and building that do not place them in essential opposition to time.[5]

During our interview, when I asked for examples of such buildings, one case Harries described is Onkel Toms Hütte, a housing complex of row houses and low-rise apartment buildings in Berlin, designed by Bruno Taut in 1932:

Bruno Taut, Onkel Toms Hütte, Berlin, 1932

This housing complex of three-storey apartment buildings and row houses built for the working class is set among trees, along winding paths and curving streets. The varied colours, asymmetrical windows, differing doors and the lush landscape stand in sharp contrast to the homogeneity and standardisation of most Modernist housing. In choosing to paint the buildings, Taut not only sought warmth and vitality, rejecting the idealised purity of the favoured white of Modernists, but also anticipated the buildings' deterioration over time, which new coats of paint could help redress, as they have.

Edward F Knowles, Langhorne Pavilion, Vieques, Puerto Rico, 1995

By intention, this small writing and sleeping pavilion, designed for Karsten Harries and his wife, 'creates a presencing of time'. An oculus brings in the changing light of the sun and the moon while also offering a view of the stars. Morning and evening light enter through generous doors facing east and west. The unpainted concrete surface, both indoors and out, visibly ages with time.

When I visited it, the following impressed me especially: How well this *Siedlung* had aged; the use of colour; the modest human scale; the small, but lovely gardens; the variety achieved with very simple means; the *Siedlung*'s integration into what is the edge of the Grunewald.

In studying images of the housing and reading about it, it becomes apparent that regular repainting of the buildings may be a significant reason for the continued attractiveness of the complex, as is the ongoing care of the landscape. Instead of choosing the perceived purity of shades of white so favoured by proponents of Modernism and assumed to remain pristine, without maintenance, Taut chose a variety of highly saturated colours for the building surfaces, doors and windows, ensuring the need for repainting.

Another example Harries described is the small Langhorne Pavilion for sleeping and writing on the island of Vieques in Puerto Rico, designed by Long Island-based architect Edward F Knowles in 1995. An oculus allows the space to be a 'sun-, moon-, and star-dial, mediating life-time and world time', giving views in the night of constellations and the changing light of the moon on the floor and walls. Generous doors to the east bring in intense morning sun: 'This active light activates the whole building, making it more substantial.' Harries continued: 'the small building creates a "presencing of time".' In this example the concrete walls, inside and out, remain unpainted so that they can change as the building ages. The pavilion, among rocks and between two mango trees 'embraces the landscape'. In *The Ethical Function of Architecture* he writes: 'A pair of trees standing firmly before a house bathe it in an aura of continuity and thus help banish the terror of time.'[6]

Notably for 'designing with time in mind' the pavilion's 'interior … opens to the time of this landscape, marked by the sun, rising and setting, by the repeating rhythm of light and dark, by the rhythms of growth and decay, of birth and death'. These observations echo similar comments made in this issue of △ regarding the value of the visceral experiences of diurnal cycles and how design can generate such experiences. The architecture below and against the tower in Bruegel's painting, the buildings and landscape of Onkel Toms Hütte and the Langhorne Pavilion display several common features. The structures are modest in size; they are placed and designed in ways that relate to what is nearby and, in the case of the pavilion, to the sun and the sky, and how changes in time can be experienced. These features help answer the question Harries poses: 'Is it necessary to think that beauty is in fundamental opposition to time?'[7]

The concrete walls, inside and out, remain unpainted so that they can change as the building ages. The pavilion, among rocks and between two mango trees 'embraces the landscape'.

MORE DIFFICULTIES, MORE POSSIBILITIES

However, another means of resisting time is through creating experiences of beauty that suspend a person's feeling that time is passing – an experience that 'is as if it had no duration'.[8] Such a definition of beauty is achievable with painting and sculpture, but when adopted it leads to 'dreams of an uninhabitable structure',[9] making architecture a 'merely aesthetic presence'.[10] A self-sufficient object of beauty cannot provide shelter; it cannot domesticate space, as so well portrayed in Thomas Cole's painting *The Architect's Dream* (1840), illustrated on page 16 of this issue.

In both his essay and book, Harries refers to a 'perennial Platonism' long evident in architecture that serves as a means to 'cope with the terror of time by spiritualizing the environment, by remaking what is sensible and changeable in the image of a higher, timeless reality'. Simple geometric forms, straight lines, right angles, regular polygons, such as a circle drawn with a compass, come 'as close as a visual statement can to the timeless realm of the spirit, while an 'expressive squiggle' has an organic look and seems to embrace time. In this tradition beauty lies in inorganic, geometric forms – a beauty that, unlike that of animals, belongs to the spirit and not the body. Harries contrasts the organic approach of the Baroque with the 'classical' approach also apparent in Modernism: 'The former invites metaphors that suggest absence, change, life, time; the latter invokes metaphors that suggest presence, stasis, death, eternity.'[11]

In cities today, replete with tall, imposing buildings that not only adopt the orthogonal grid, but also relentlessly proclaim it throughout the skyline, we may lose touch with the alternatives Harries describes, and possibly also with the organic qualities inherent in life, in time and in our own bodies. This contrast between the extent and power of the orthogonal grids of city skylines and the more organic shapes that are possible, but for now far less prevalent, is apparent in a view from Governors Island, New York, during the summer of 2015. Here one sees the buildings of Lower Manhattan in the background, and trees and BanG studio's Billion Oyster Pavilion (see pages 106–7) in the foreground.

Sharing another perspective with contributors to this issue of △, Harries recognises the value of an architecture that can be quickly assembled and disassembled: 'Do we not need more flexible solutions, solutions that will accommodate an inevitably open future with its new desires and associations?' He extends this idea:

> A dynamic counter-image to the traditional city emerges: a city held together by a relative stable support structure that would take care of plumbing electricity, communication and the like but would allow for maximum flexibility with respect to the location and nature of dwelling.[12]

BanG studio,
Billion Oyster Pavilion,
FIGMENT City of Dreams,
Governors Island,
New York,
summer 2015

The organic, expressive form of the pavilion and shapes of the nearby trees stand in dramatic contrast to the inorganic, geometric facades of the buildings of Lower Manhattan, replete with orthogonal grids, with two slight variations: the faceted sides of One World Trade Center and the pyramid atop the Woolworth Building.

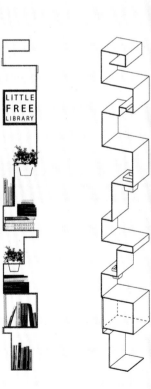

Design Studio III/
Irwin S Chanin School
of Architecture,
A Little Free Library,
The Cooper Union,
New York,
May–September 2013

One of 10 winning entries in a competition for mini-libraries sponsored by the Architectural League of New York and the PEN World Voices Festival, these steel-frame book stacks were installed in the voids between pairs of columns in the portico of the building. The frame is intended to be adaptable to different sites and conditions, and instructions are available online through the Architectural League for doing so. Design studio leaders: Maja Hjertén Knutson and Christopher Taleff; Faculty team: Michael Young, David Allin and Lydia Kallipoliti.

Although none of the other contributors make such a wide-ranging proposal, their work does illustrate the impermanent and the flexible, and they do question the privileging of a static architecture that seeks to resist time and sees beauty only in the untouched and unoccupied. Indeed, some of the installations illustrated in the issue are much more like the dwellings nestled against the tower in Bruegel's painting, or the city below, than the tower itself. They join a growing popularity of small-scale, temporary insertions in urban public space that meet everyday needs for leisure, education and community, made by designers and by citizens. One example is free, public mini-libraries.

At the end of the interview, the conversation took a different turn. When Harries was asked whether his ideas about architecture and time have changed, he replied that he did not previously 'think of space as a scarce resource' and that the tendency to take 'time and space for granted' needs to change. Despite a deteriorating environment and the depletion of clean water, air and soil, 'our responses remain half-hearted'. While he acknowledged that green architecture is one positive response, space itself 'needs to be considered a scarce resource that architects have to learn to stop wasting … no doubt in response to clients who demand big and excessive'. And so a 'rethinking of time' is needed: 'The future needs to be given a weight that for most Americans it now does not possess. We have to learn that our lives become hollow when we no longer look ahead and care for our children and children's children and coming generations.'

OTHER TRADITIONS AND INTENTIONS, OTHER OUTCOMES

A rereading of Harries's essay following our conversations suggested that architecture's responses to the terror of time he describes might be Western in origin and influence. Traditions in other cultures might be far less likely to generate the same idealisation of formal geometric, inorganic forms and the desire for the presumed permanence of monumental, weighty structures that never change in reaction to time or use. In Japan, for instance, age-old beliefs privilege not permanence and stasis, but renewal and the repeated remaking of space both at a domestic scale of movable screens and household furnishings, and also at the collective scale of the rebuilding of shrines. And, in the continuing context of Buddhist ideas, the change of seasons is celebrated, and the passing of time and inevitability of decay and mortality are acknowledged, giving great significance to the present moment.[13] Indeed, contemporary Japanese architecture, including the work of Toyo Ito, presents examples that illustrate these and other traditions and intentions.

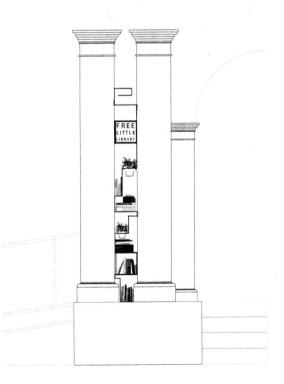

In talking about one of his most well-known buildings, the Sendai Mediatheque, Japanese architect Toyo Ito recalled that in Nagano, where he grew up, four wooden pillars define the sacred space of the Suwa Taisha shrine. Every six years the villagers chop down four trees in the nearby mountains to replace the pillars and so to preserve the energy that is believed to emanate from them.[14] Ito acknowledges the connection between trees and the tubes that figure significantly in the Mediatheque, but also, as Ito has said elsewhere, he welcomes the possible changes in events and

Toyo Ito,
Sendai Mediatheque,
Miyagi,
Japan,
2001

right: Thirteen 'tubes', which
penetrate the flat concrete slabs
(or 'plates') house a variety of
building functions and serve as
the main dividers of the space
on each floor. The minimising of
interior walls allows for a freedom
of functions and programming in
the spaces between the tubes. The
three main elements of plate, tube
and skin allow for great flexibility
for new programmes and different
uses of spaces in the future.

below middle: The ground floor
opens to the outside with a café
shop and public square; the
first floor offers newspapers,
magazines and computers; the
second and third are open stacks;
the fourth and fifth house gallery
spaces; and the sixth is for viewing
and creating visual media.

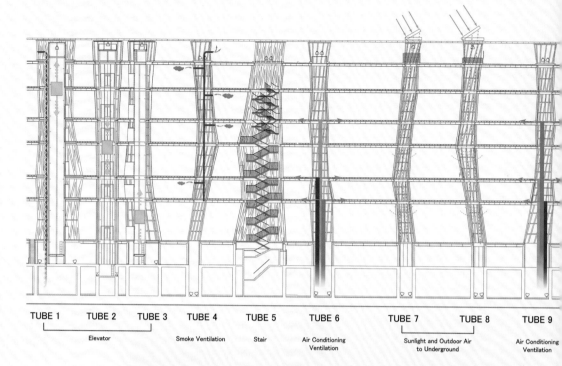

TUBE 1	TUBE 2	TUBE 3	TUBE 4	TUBE 5	TUBE 6	TUBE 7	TUBE 8	TUBE 9
Elevator			Smoke Ventilation	Stair	Air Conditioning Ventilation	Sunlight and Outdoor Air to Underground		Air Conditioning Ventilation

Ito believes architecture has distanced people from nature and he seeks to re-establish what was once an intimate relationship.

Toyo Ito,
Tama Art University
Library,
Hachioji,
Tokyo,
2007

A structural system
composed of steel plates
placed between two layers
of concrete allows the
concrete arches of the
ground-floor public areas
to be of minimal thickness
and the cross joint columns
to have an extremely thin
form. The interior spaces are
continuous, divided only
by the crisscrossing of the
arches.

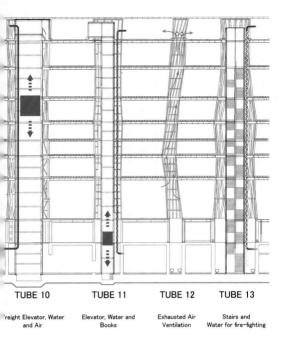

TUBE 10 TUBE 11 TUBE 12 TUBE 13

Freight Elevator, Water and Air · Elevator, Water and Books · Exhausted Air Ventilation · Stairs and Water for fire-fighting

programmed activities that the open spaces between the tubes support. Indeed, rather than seeing the beauty of a building in all its pristine emptiness, Ito sees its beauty in human presence: 'I have always intended to design architecture to look more beautiful with humans present.'[15]

When an interviewer asked him if Japanese traditions influence his work, Ito recalled former cherry blossom festivals where people 'went into a park, into nature, and separated a certain area underneath the trees with draperies. By doing nothing more than that, they created a special place. This way of thinking – that a simple drapery is enough to separate yourself from nature, is very Japanese and important in my work.'[16]

And so it is: as Ito himself and many others have recognised, his buildings are light on the earth. With regard to the concerns raised in this article, they make no attempt to dominate space or time in its size or in materiality. One can see one source for the lightness, airiness and fabric-like quality of Ito's architecture in his statement: 'When I think about architecture, I think of it as a piece of clothing that must be wrapped around human beings.'[17] And, in some cases, the building actually moves: the 13 tubes in the Mediatheque gave the building flexibility, allowing it to move and so survive the devastating earthquake of 2011.

Ito believes architecture has distanced people from nature and he seeks to re-establish what was once an intimate relationship – when natural conditions of sun, wind and light shaped architectural forms. And he wishes to create experiences of nature for the occupants of his buildings. The tree-like tubes of the Sendai Mediatheque are intended to re-create an experience of being in a forest; when people enter his completely solar-powered stadium in Kaohsiung, Taiwan (2009), he wants them to be able to feel the wind and the air.

Ito sees that one step towards creating a closer relationship between nature and architecture (and thereby people) is to recognise the power and the deficiencies of the classical geometric shapes and the orthogonal grid, adopted as 'an absolute order against the world of natural phenomena', and to discover instead an order found in natural organisms that is not absolute, but changes. This new order would be 'fluid', 'relative, flexible and soft' and influenced by external factors, much as the growth of a tree is affected, based on instability and change. One possibility is patterns where lines do not intersect orthogonally, but at obtuse and acute angles.[18]

Ito's intentions and the resultant architecture present dramatic alternatives to Western traditions in architecture and their consequences, as depicted, for example, in Nancy Wolf's *Prisoner to a Grid* (1973), shown on page 8 of this issue and Cole's *The Architect's Dream*. An architecture that is no longer beholden to the orthogonal grid, that no longer seeks to overcome time or to oppose nature, that aims to invite human activities and to support how they change, is no longer built in a terror of time. ᗕ

Notes
1. Karsten Harries, 'Building and the Terror of Time', *Perspecta: The Yale Architecture Journal*, 19, 1982, pp 59–69.
2. Karsten Harries, *The Ethical Function of Architecture*, MIT Press (Cambridge, MA), 1998.
3. Harries, 'Building and the Terror of Time', *op cit*, p 60.
4. *Ibid*, p 69.
5. *Ibid*, p 69.
6. Harries, *The Ethical Function of Architecture*, *op cit*, p 221.
7. Harries, 'Building and the Terror of Time', *op cit*, p 66.
8. *Ibid*, p 64.
9. *Ibid*, p 65.
10. *Ibid*, p 66.
11. Harries, *The Ethical Function of Architecture*, *op cit*, p 228.
12. *Ibid*, p 250.
13. Kevin Nute, *Place, Time and Being in Japanese Architecture*, Routledge (London), 2004.
14. Claudia Hildner, 'Interview: Toyo Ito', *The Architectural Review*, 22 March 2013: www.architectural-review.com/view/interview-toyo-ito/8644601.article.
15. Movie interview: Toyo Ito on architecture as a piece of clothing, *Dezeen*, 31 July 2014: www.dezeen.com/2014/07/31/movie-interview-toyo-ito-architecture-clothing-wrap-around-human-beings/.
16. Hildner, *op cit*.
17. Movie interview: Toyo Ito, *op cit*.
18. Toyo Ito, 'In Search of a New Architectural Order', in Toyo Ito, Riken Yamamoto, Dana Buntrock and Taro Igarashi, *Toyo Ito*, Phaidon Press (London), 2009, p 8.

Finding Time

COUNTERPOINT 01/2016 No 239

Tim Makower

What has our sense of the acceleration of time got to bear on our experience of cities? How might it be consciously countered by architects 'finding time' through 'thoughtful design and measured observation'. A self-declared 'cultural polymath', **Tim Makower** is the founder of Makower Architects. A partner at Allies and Morrison for many years, he has significant experience in leading large-scale projects, ranging from the King's Cross Masterplan in London to the Old Doha Regeneration Framework, which he draws on here and in his book *Touching the City: Thoughts on Urban Scale* (Wiley, 2014).

We dwell in time as much as in space, and architecture mediates equally our relationship with this mysterious dimension, giving it its human measure.
— Juhani Pallasmaa, 'Inhabiting Time', see pp 50–59

The desire to catch the moment and to leave something behind us is part of the creative process. It results in products of creativity; objects that are outside of ourselves, and that to some extent have a life of their own. A piece of architecture is different from a tune, a poem or a painting in that it generally arises from the needs of third parties – a living client with a living brief. This is a significant part of its temporal dimension; the push and pull of design and construction, and the hard realities of a design team working in a competitive environment 'finding time'. Indeed, it is easy to disagree with Friedrich von Schelling's mantra that 'Architecture is frozen music'[1] because frozen is something it never is.

The pursuit of time surfaces in this issue in two themes that run between the essays: firstly the dynamic nature of architecture; and secondly the continual overlap between the process and product of design as a factor, and a vector, of time. It can be argued that the creative process stems from the desire (the need) to externalise what is within us, and thereby to a greater or lesser degree, to defy time; to challenge mortality even. Time expands and contracts and, like the flow of traffic on a highway it accelerates and decelerates, at least in our perception. Sometimes, when empty, a day can seem to drag. When full, a week can feel like a day in the present, and a month when looking back.

The aim of this Counterpoint, 'Finding Time', in contrast to what has already been written, is to examine three aspects of our experience of time in cities that are fundamentally part of our perception of the urban environment and, for those who are involved in architecture or urban design, should inform our thoughts and actions as designers: firstly newness, speed and finance; secondly the patina of age; and thirdly the temporary and ephemeral stuff of cities.

Central Business District, West Bay, Doha, Qatar, 2012

Doha's West Bay is a good example of 'fast urbanism'; like fast food it seems to lack substance. But unlike food, as a piece of city, it can continue to mature from generation to generation, and improve with age, even though its individual buildings alienate themselves from their context in terms of culture and climate.

I Want it New and I Want it Now

The all too familiar challenge of vast-scale, fast-track developments creating urban environments with shallow (or no) roots, with scant chance of improving with age, is compounded by the fact that it is often cheaper to throw buildings away and build new ones than to retain and renew old ones.

It is a dead end, however, to look back with nostalgia at the days when development was on a smaller scale, and slower. Market forces are natural; they are like lifeblood pumping in a body. As designers we should embrace them as an essential part of the development process, but focus with ever-increasing insightfulness on the product of what we are creating and how it is experienced, not by us as designers but by the public, who have no knowledge or interest in design, other than their own perception and intuition. If developments such as West Bay – Doha's Central Business District – can be created in less than a decade, the question is not 'how can it be slowed down?'. Rather we must ask 'how can we emulate those aspects of the slow-grown city that we enjoy, and which are beneficial to individuals and communities?'. The desire to develop fast and on a large scale is not in itself negative; the question is how.

As Kevin Lynch has pointed out: 'At the present tempo of building, there is not time for the slow adjustment of form to small, individualized forces. Therefore we must depend far more than formerly on conscious design: the deliberate manipulation of the world for sensuous ends.'[2]

The term 'urban picturesque' is not much used, but is indeed the key to satisfying both the crude forces of time and money, and the more refined sensibilities of designers, planners, visionaries and, of course, of the person on the street. When a large-scale high-speed project brings dehumanising degrees of repetition or regularity, Lynch's 'conscious design' can step in to irregularise; to patinate the urban realm, even if it is all new. If intellectuals worry that the picturesque veers towards the inauthentic or irrational, they need to explain what is 'rational' about creating a place that is monotonous or alienating, and redefine their terms.

As we know, time is money, and building fast is often treated as a priority of the highest order. Incremental phasing, however, is also a key to success. The ability to go slow – to wait, to catch the wave, to balance supply and demand – is an essential part of sustainable development in the economic environment to achieve the long-term success without which other aspects of sustainable design would be foundationless.

While a conscious use of picturesque urbanism is necessary to humanise large all-new developments, another essential tool is a robust and flexible framework, broken down into small pieces that can be developed over many years (or all at once) and can to some extent take on a life of their own – organised chaos. My own experience of two major masterplans – those for London's King's Cross and Msheireb in Doha that I led as a partner with Allies and Morrison, both 800,000-square-metre (8.6 million-square-foot) mixed-use projects that are now more than half complete – exemplifies the need to divide and subdivide. Of the two, Msheireb is more literally like history speeded up, but the fact that many architects have been used over a multilayered

Argent,
Allies and Morrison and Porphyrios,
King's Cross Masterplan,
London,
due for completion 2020

above: The King's Cross urban regeneration masterplan was designed specifically to be able to go fast or slow – in response to the property market – without jeopardising its commercial success. The flexibility of most of the northern blocks (right-hand side of the model) to be built over time as either residential or office space was also an essential part of its responsive financial model.

Allies and Morrison,
National Archive and Radwani House,
Msheireb,
Doha, Qatar,
due for completion 2018

below: Msheireb as a masterplan was an extreme case of 'history speeded up', with an intricate woven plan of 800,000 square metres (8.6 million square feet) being designed and built in less than a decade. Nevertheless, many of its buildings, such as the National Archive, are embedded among original buildings and historical street patterns.

Makower Architects,
Zones 15 and 16,
Al Ghanem-Jadeeda Development Framework,
Doha,
Qatar,
2015

The heritage-led regeneration framework for this run-down old neighbourhood in central Doha proposes a strategy for 'patchwork repair' of an established streetscape. Its historical fabric is retained, renewed, augmented and enriched with a combination of new and old structures, at both large and small scales.

plan ensures that a fine degree of complexity and character can still be achieved. A robust plan will enable development to move fast, but will not be ruined by it if it does, provided it enables architectural packages to be broken down into 'bite-size chunks'.

On the Beauty of Ageing

I was brought up on the assumption that old buildings were better than new ones. New ones were just 'too new'. It took a while to acknowledge that buildings are commodities and that, like cars, new ones are generally preferred to second-hand.

There is of course nothing wrong with newness in buildings, provided they are designed to age well, and old buildings and streets, with their special textures and atmospheres, are not thoughtlessly thrown away to make space for the new without an understanding of their qualities and their value. It is an ideal for most people to 'age gracefully', and the same can be said of buildings.

In terms of ageing, there are three kinds of buildings. Firstly, those that degrade with age; their material, their fabric and their resonance diminish. Secondly, those that seem not to age; they are impervious, splendidly unresponsive to external influences. Thirdly, the ideal – for the long-term benefit of city making – is to create buildings that get better with age, century after century.

Henry Cole Wing,
Victoria and Albert Museum,
Exhibition Road,
London,
2012

The shrapnel scars from the Second
World War have been left on the
stonework of the V&A as a living piece
of urban memory. It is good when
buildings can absorb and assimilate
the lichens, erosions and patinations
of time – and even bomb blasts
sometimes – as part of their natural
ageing process within the city.

It is a shame if the value
of a piece of design is lost
through the ageing process

Even scars, sometimes traumatic, can be part of the quality of a building. The Exhibition Road facade of London's Victoria and Albert Museum is blasted with shrapnel wounds from the Blitz, and this is indeed part of its quality, both on the surface and within. Interestingly, this will be lost with the new scheme now under construction – will this bring with it a loss of memory?

The beauty and patina of urban ageing has no equivalent. Cities, unlike people, do not die due to ageing. If properly looked after, they can continue to get better and better into the future without limit. The masterplan for Al Ghanem-Jadeeda in Doha, where Makower Architects is setting out a heritage-led regeneration plan for the local authority, is an immediate challenge in terms of embracing the ageing process and making a 'collage city' possible. This is an area – the size of London's Soho and Covent Garden combined – where uncontrolled low-grade development is leading fast to the destruction of one of Doha's last largely intact historic neighbourhoods. Our aim is to redefine the meaning of the word 'value', helping landowners to realise that financial and cultural 'value' overlaps and is multiplied if a long-term, more complex view is taken. A carefully balanced combination of large- and small-scale developments, and both old and new building fabric, offers an equivalent of the current free-for-all in quantitative terms, but something of infinitely more profound and significant value in terms of quality.

I have likened the saving of historical fabric, and promoting bold contemporary interventions in existing buildings, to using an expensive spice to make a tasty meal. It costs more in time and money initially, albeit in small quantities, but gives far greater value in the long term, as evoked by Jane Jacobs:

> Cities need old buildings so badly it is probably impossible for vigorous streets and districts to grow without them. By old buildings I mean not museum-piece old buildings, … in an excellent and expensive state of rehabilitation – although these make fine ingredients – but also a good lot of plain, ordinary, low-value old buildings, including some rundown ones.[3]

Before moving on from the subject of ageing, we must mention the idea of timelessness. This hard-to-define notion has been raised several times in the essays of this issue of △, but not specifically in relation to ageing, or fashion. Fashion is defined by the Oxford English Dictionary as 'the latest style'. It is by nature passing. It is a shame if the value of a piece of design is lost through the ageing process and thus it is desirable to transcend fashion, even when embracing it. Is it a noble goal to achieve an architecture that is neither old-fashioned nor fashionable? Is this timelessness?

Breathe Deeply

A third aspect of time as we experience it in architecture and urbanism, which is easy to forget, and is not easy to take account of as a designer, is the ephemeral or passing aspects of the built environment. As designers we often think the ephemeral is not our concern. However, the cafe facade that folds away when the weather is good, the array of shopfronts

Regent Street,
London,
2015

A street that is closed to traffic
for only four days a year takes on
a new dimension in the memory
of those who experience it in its
pedestrian-only state, whereby a
new sense of belonging is created.
The change is as dramatic in the
life of the city as it would be if
a street were roofed over and
became a forum or an agora, even
if just for a moment.

alive with change and bristling with the cacophony of competing businesses, and the street that is pedestrianised once a month in the summer; these things are like the city breathing.

It is easy to think of architecture as a process of defining things with a physical fabric, but often it is better to blur the boundaries between the designed and un-designed, and treat the design of buildings as a beginning rather than an end. As Guest-Editor Karen A Franck states in her introduction to this issue: 'Embracing time in architecture means embracing change.'[4]

The seasonal quality of a city and the changing life-patterns of buildings underpin and oversail their forms, their spaces and their surfaces, becoming over time as much part of their nature as the bricks, concrete or glass from which they are made.

Fast Living, Measured Thinking

In conclusion, while history is being speeded up, a complementary parallel process of thoughtful design and intense observation will enable time to be slowed down in the minds and drawing hands of those of us who design cities. We only have to look hard at the combinations of old and new, large and small, temporary and permanent, and fast and slow in the streets and spaces that surround us to find clues towards emulating time in urbanism, whether this is by allowing the city to evolve on its own, or with a conscious use of the urban picturesque.

When considering buildings, and groups of buildings that make up the streets and spaces of the city, it is important to think of perception and memory before we think of substance; to operate as part of a collective rather than as an individual, in order to engage fully with time, that 'mysterious dimension, which gives architecture its human measure'.[5] On this basis, it is reasonable to say that there is no perfection without imperfection, no purity without impurity, and no reason without a good measure of the intuitive, and often the irrational too. ᴆ

> Embracing time in architecture means embracing change.
> – Karen Frank

Notes

1. Friedrich von Schelling, *Die Weltalter, 1811–15 (The Ages of the World),* trans Frederick de Wolfe Bolman, Jr, Columbia University Press (New York), 1967, p 163.
2. Kevin Lynch, *The Image of the City,* MIT Press (Cambridge, MA and London), 1960, p 116.
3. Jane Jacobs, *The Death and Life of Great American Cities,* Random House (New York), 1961, p 187.
4. Karen A Franck, 'Designing with Time in Mind', see pp 8–17 of this issue.
5. Juhani Pallasmaa, 'Inhabiting Time', see pp 50–59 of this issue.

CONTRIBUTORS

△ ARCHITECTURAL DESIGN

ARCHITECTURE TIMED

Tobias Armborst is an architect and urban designer. He is Principal and co-founder of the New York City-based architecture, planning and research office Interboro Partners, as well as Associate Professor of Art and Urban Studies at Vassar College. He received a Master of Architecture in Urban Design from Harvard Graduate School of Design (GSD) and a Diplom-Ingenieur from the Rheinisch-Westfälische Technische Hochschule Aachen, Germany.

Babak Bryan is a founding partner of BanG studio, and an LEED-accredited registered architect. In 2011 he was recognised by *Engineering News Record* as one of the 'top 20 under 40' construction professionals in the New York Metro region. With a degree in engineering from the University of California, Berkeley and a Master of Architecture from Columbia University, he seeks a balance between technical rigour and critical insight. He is currently an adjunct assistant professor at Columbia University, and has taught at the University of Pennsylvania and the City College of New York,

Martina Decker is an assistant professor in the College of Architecture and Design at the New Jersey Institute of Technology (NJIT). She is originally from Munich, where she received her professional architecture degree from the University of Applied Sciences. She has worked on a wide range of award-winning projects that show her penchant for interdisciplinary work, including art installations, consumer products and buildings. She pursues design innovation through the exploration of emergent materials, working directly with various types of smart materials and nano-materials. At NJIT, she continues her interdisciplinary endeavours in her Material Dynamics Lab.

Daniel D'Oca is an urban planner. He is Principal and co-founder of Interboro Partners. He is also Design Critic in Urban Planning and Design at Harvard GSD, where he received a Master in Urban Planning degree.

Richard Garber is Director of the School of Architecture at NJIT and a partner at the New York practice GRO Architects. He uses computer simulation and numerically controlled hardware to generate innovative design, construction and assembly solutions. He has published two volumes with John Wiley & Sons: △ *Closing the Gap: Information Models in Contemporary Design Practice* (2009); and a book, *BIM Design: Realising the Creative Potential of Building Information Modelling* (2014).

Federica Goffi is Associate Professor and Associate Director of Graduate Programs at the Azrieli School of Architecture and Urbanism at Carleton University in Ottawa. She was previously Assistant Professor at the Rhode Island School of Design. She holds a PhD in Architectural Design and Representation from Virginia Tech. She is the author of *Time Matter[s]: Invention and Re-imagination in Built Conservation – The Unfinished Drawing and Building of St Peter's, the Vatican* (Ashgate, 2013). Her articles investigating the concept of time in its threefold nature of time-weather-tempo have appeared in *ARQ, In.Form, Interstices* and *Int.AR*. She is a licensed architect in her native country, Italy.

Henry Grosman is a founding partner of BanG studio. He received his BA in Computer Science from Columbia University, and his MArch from the Columbia University Graduate School of Architecture, Planning, and Preservation (GSAPP). He has worked in such diverse fields as interactive media, game design and telecommunications. He has taught at Parsons School of Design in New York, as well as at Columbia. He is currently a co-coordinator of second-year design studios at NJIT. His academic and design work explores the intricate relationship between emerging computational techniques and design culture.

Brian McGrath is an architect and founder of urban-interface, which fuses expertise in urban design, ecology and media. His books include the △ Reader *Urban Design Ecologies* (John Wiley & Sons, 2012), *Digital Modelling and Urban Design* (John Wiley & Sons, 2008) and *Transparent Cities* (Lumen, 1994). *Resilience in Ecology and Urban Design* (Springer, 2012) was co-edited with ecologists Steward Pickett and Mary Cadenasso; *Cinemetrics: Architectural Drawing Today* (John Wiley & Sons, 2007) was co-authored with Jean Gardner; and his △ *Sensing the 21st Century City: Close-Up and Remote* (2006) was co-edited with David Grahame Shane. He is currently Dean of the School of Constructed Environments and Professor of Urban Design at Parsons School of Design in New York.

Tim Makower is an architect, urbanist and cultural polymath, educated at Cambridge and the Royal College of Art (RCA). He is the founder of Makower Architects, an international practice specialising in architecture and urbanism. Projects include several major residential schemes in London and Cambridge, a listed boat house, the Al Rayyan Gate masterplan, Old Doha Regeneration Framework and the GORD Eco Villa. As a partner in his previous practice he led many projects, including the King's Cross Masterplan, St Andrew's Bow, Liverpool One, Msheireb and the Qatar National Archive. He was chair of architecture in Qatar, has published numerous articles on architecture and the urban realm, is the author of *Touching the City: Thoughts on Urban Scale* (John Wiley & Sons, 2014), and the founder of the '10x10 Drawing the City' exhibition and auction.

Jonathan Mallie is the founder of JLM | design & construction consultancy, and focuses on the integration of design innovation with technologically advanced construction solutions. Previously, as a Principal of SHoP and the Managing Principal of SC, he held key leadership positions on the Porter House in New York, the Barclays Center arena in Brooklyn, the MBB Tower in Miami, and the renovation of the Nassau Coliseum on Long Island. Jonathan received his Bachelor of Science in Design from the University of Florida, and a Master of Architecture, with Honours for Excellence in Design, from Columbia University.

Kevin Nute is a professor of architecture at the University of Oregon. He trained at the Universities of Nottingham and Cambridge, and has been a Fulbright Scholar at the University of California, Berkeley and a Japan Foundation Fellow at the University of Tokyo. He is the author of *Frank Lloyd Wright and Japan* (Van Nostrand, 1993) – winner of a 1994 AIA International Monograph Award – as well as *Place, Time and Being in Japanese Architecture* (Routledge, 2004) and, most recently, *Vital: Using the Weather to Bring Buildings and Sustainability to Life* (Apple iBookstore, 2014).

Juhani Pallasmaa, architect and professor emeritus, has worked in urban, architectural, exhibition, product and graphic design. He has held several positions, including Professor and Dean at the Helsinki University of Technology, Director of the Museum of Finnish Architecture, and Rector of the Institute of Industrial Arts, Helsinki. He has been a visiting professor in several notable universities in the US, and lectured around the world. He has published 45 books, and received several Finnish and international prizes and honours for architecture and criticism.

Eric Parry established Eric Parry Architects in 1983. Under his leadership, the practice has developed a reputation for delivering beautifully crafted and well-considered buildings that respond to their context. London has been the focus and the setting for most of his work. He was elected Royal Academician (RA) in 2006 and awarded the honorary degree of Doctor of Arts from the University of Bath in 2012. He has served on the Arts Council of England's Visual Arts and Architecture panel, chaired the Royal Academy Architecture Committee and the RIBA Awards Group, and was President of the Architectural Association (AA).

Philip Speranza is an assistant professor in the School of Architecture and Allied Arts at the University of Oregon and directs the Life, City, Adaptation: Barcelona Urban Design Program. He holds a Master of Architecture from Columbia University, a Bachelor of Science in Architecture with minor in Philosophy from the University of Virginia, and is a practising architect. Design projects in the US and Spain have included urban design, public art works with artist Janet Echelman, infrastructure, mixed-use and housing. His research interest in urban design and computing investigates new geographic information workflows using in-situ data collection of urban phenomena.

Jill Stoner has been a professor of architecture for 35 years, the last 28 of which she has spent at the University of California, Berkeley. She is currently Director of the Azrieli School of Architecture and Urbanism at Carleton University in Ottawa. Her professional practice (1993–2007), devoted to the adaptive reuse of public buildings and visionary competitions, received national and international awards. Her first book, *Poems for Architects* (William Stout Publishers, 2001) investigates the spatial sensibility of the 20th century through a collection of modern poems. Her more recent book, *Toward a Minor Architecture* (MIT Press, 2012) advocates for a more political approach to the post-recession landscape.

Mark Taylor is Professor of Architecture at the University of Newcastle, Australia. He is an editorial advisor to *Interiors: Design, Architecture, Culture*, and regularly reviews papers and book manuscripts for international publishers. His writing on the interior has been widely published in journals and book chapters, He was the guest-editor of △ *Surface Consciousness* (2003), and editor of *Intimus: Interior Design Theory Reader* (John Wiley & Sons, 2006), the four-volume anthology *Interior Design and Architecture: Critical and Primary Sources* (2013) and, with Anca Lasc and Georgina Downey, of *Designing the French Interior: The Modern Home and Mass Media* (2015), both published by Bloomsbury.

Georgeen Theodore is an architect and urban designer. She is Principal and co-founder of Interboro Partners. She is also Associate Professor at the NJIT College of Architecture and Design, where she is the Director of the Infrastructure Planning programme. She received a Bachelor of Architecture from Rice University in Houston, and a Master of Architecture in Urban Design from Harvard GSD.

SueAnne Ware is Head of the School of Architecture and the Built Environment at the University of Newcastle, Australia. She holds a Master's degree in landscape architecture from the University of California, Berkeley and a PhD from RMIT University, Melbourne. Her most recent books include *Sunburnt: Australian Practices of Landscape Architecture* (Sun, 2011), edited with Julian Raxworthy, and *Taylor Cullity Lethlean: Making Sense of Landscape* (SpaceMaker, 2013), edited with Gini Lee. Her research outputs as creative works (the SIEV X memorial, Road as Shrine, and Anti-Memorial to Heroin Overdose Victims) have won international awards from the Australian Institute of Landscape Architecture.

What is Architectural Design?

Founded in 1930, *Architectural Design* (△) is an influential and prestigious publication. It combines the currency and topicality of a newsstand journal with the rigour and production qualities of a book. With an almost unrivalled reputation worldwide, it is consistently at the forefront of cultural thought and design.

Each title of △ is edited by an invited Guest-Editor, who is an international expert in the field. Renowned for being at the leading edge of design and new technologies, △ also covers themes as diverse as architectural history, the environment, interior design, landscape architecture and urban design.

Provocative and inspirational, △ inspires theoretical, creative and technological advances. It questions the outcome of technical innovations as well as the far-reaching social, cultural and environmental challenges that present themselves today.

For further information on △, subscriptions and purchasing single issues see:

www.architectural-design-magazine.com

Volume 85 No 1
ISBN 978 1118 759066

Volume 85 No 2
ISBN 978 1118 700570

Volume 85 No 3
ISBN 978 1118 829011

Volume 85 No 4
ISBN 978 1118 914830

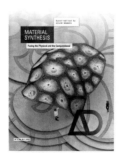

Volume 85 No 5
ISBN 978 1118 878378

Volume 85 No 6
ISBN 978 1118 915646